How to Stop Hating and Start Loving

Born in New York City in 1928, Jack Birnbaum moved to Toronto as a child. He graduated in medicine from the University of Toronto in 1952, continued his medical studies at Mount Sinai Hospital, Cleveland, Ohio, and went on to practise general medicine in Toronto for ten years.

In 1963 Dr Birnbaum entered the field of psychiatry, studying at the Institute of Living, Hartford, Connecticut, and at the Clarke Institute of Psychiatry in Toronto. He is now a member of the staff of York University, Toronto, and also has a private psychiatric practice. Dr Birnbaum is married and has four children.

Jack Birnbaum MD FRCP(C)

How to Stop Hating and Start Loving

Pan Books in association with
William Heinemann

ACKNOWLEDGEMENTS – From Edith Fowke, *Sally Go Round the Sun*,
© McClelland & Stewart Ltd 1969 and reprinted by permission of the
Canadian publishers, McClelland & Stewart Ltd,
Toronto, and of Doubleday & Company Inc, New York
From Dylan Thomas, *The Poems of Dylan Thomas*,
copyright Dylan Thomas 1952 and reprinted by permission of
New Directions Publishing Corp, J. M. Dent & Sons Ltd,
J. M. Dent & Sons (Canada) Ltd and the Trustees
for the copyrights of the late Dylan Thomas

First published in Great Britain 1975 by William Heinemann Ltd
This edition published 1977 by Pan Books Ltd,
Cavaye Place, London SW10 9PG,
in association with William Heinemann Ltd
© Jack Birnbaum 1973, 1975
Originally published in Canada 1973 by
General Publishing Co Ltd as *Cry Anger*
ISBN 0 330 24064 7
Printed and bound in Great Britain by
Hazell Watson & Viney Ltd, Aylesbury, Bucks

to the two men whose work most inspired me

Eric Berne and Frederick Perls

Author's note

The case histories used in this book are taken from my clinical practice in psychiatry. Names and details have been changed to protect the confidentiality of my patients.

Contents

1 The beginning

1 I am an angry psychiatrist

I am an angry psychiatrist. I reject some of the old ways of psychotherapy. Why? Simply because I know that it is no longer necessary to spend years with a patient in slow, tedious analysis of his past. The recent developments in psychotherapy can increase the effectiveness, and shorten the duration, of treatment of emotional illnesses.

If you have read Eric Berne's *Games People Play* or Thomas Harris's *I'm OK – You're OK*, you are already familiar with one of these developments, the concept of ego states. If you haven't read these books, I'd like to give you a simple explanation. The three ego states are the basic parts of your personality.

The *Parent ego state* acts as your built-in parents. It consists of your basic value system of ideals, morality and conscience. It may be critical and punitive, or nurturing and loving.

When I say 'I am an angry psychiatrist,' I hear my critical Parent telling me, 'Don't be angry! You should be nice! All doctors, especially psychiatrists, should be kind, gentle and caring. Besides, you should have better control of your feelings.'

My loving Parent says, 'I like you just because you're you. If you're angry, that's fine, for I know you'll use your anger to help yourself and others.'

The *Child ego state* is the child you were when you were young, and who is still present within you. The Child ego state is the seat of your emotions, and may be sad, happy, rebellious, frightened, angry, helpless or even sexy.

It is really my Child ego state that says, 'I am an angry psychiatrist.' He screams in my ear, 'You bet I'm angry! I hate the frustrations and pain of mental illness. I'm fed up with psychiatrists who are passive and evasive, for they belittle their patients. I want to scream at the bull-shitting and mind-fucking that passes as psychotherapy. Damn the months and years of treatment with the old therapies!'

The *Adult ego state* is a computer within you that deals with facts in a logical way. This ego state monitors the daily reality of here-and-now living. The Adult ego state thinks.

My Adult ego state hears my angry Child and reflects, 'Traditional psychotherapy has focused so much on the patient's past that it frequently ignores his present behaviour. I'll use the "Here and Now" psychologies of Eric Berne's Transactional Analysis and Fritz Perls' Gestalt Therapy to deal as intensely as

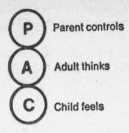

P Parent controls

A Adult thinks

C Child feels

Ego states

possible with the present. I think this will bring better results and shorten the duration of therapy as well. If the passive psychiatrist is ineffective, I'll be an active psychotherapist, using the way I feel and think openly and directly. I think that reasoning, intellectualizing, asking "why?" and seeking a "because" are usually ineffective. For most mental problems are disordered emotions, and a level of perception that stresses feeling is needed for effective behavioural change.'

As you read this book, approach it not only through your 'head', the Adult ego state of reason, logic and facts, but also through your 'gut', the eyes of the aware Child within you. We are so conditioned to thinking things out that we tend to lock out our emotional awareness. Use a different level of perception – bring in the Child ego state with its feeling, experiencing, imagery, fantasy, imagination, identification and empathy.

You and I can learn to use all our ego states, independently or together, in a spontaneous way. Above all, we can learn to use our ego states to express the one emotion that creates the most pain, guilt, anxiety and depression – *our anger*.

2 The faces of anger

2 Everyday anger

'You make me angry!'

If you believe the statement that other people can make you angry, then you really believe in voodoo magic. Other people cannot make you feel anything. Each of us, alone, is completely responsible for the way he feels. Of course, if I scream at you, you respond. However, the way you respond depends entirely on your personality and on your patterns of behaviour. If I scream at you, you may run away, cry, laugh or fight back. But whatever you do is 'you'. I did not make you feel anything.

Many patients come into my office playing the game 'If It Weren't for You', blaming their mothers, mothers-in-law, fathers, spouses, boyfriends, bosses or the government for their emotional upsets. This is probably one of the biggest cop-outs in emotional illnesses – blaming other people and things for your feelings. Let us be honest. If this were really true, then in order to make you better we would have to treat the other party or the rest of the world. Yes, I will admit that you respond to a crisis or to another person quite automatically, for example with 'depression'. Hopefully, through growth you will gain in flexibility and in freedom to express your feelings.

'I'm not sad, I'm mad!'

I am amazed at how many people cry during an expression of angry feelings. Most of the time the crying is really a mask for hostility that they have found unacceptable. As they cry, they feel sad; but, as they get in touch with the cry, they can usually experience the underlying rage. Their tears of sadness have become a denial of their hostility. This pattern usually indicates some old script that was introduced at an early age, probably from parents, and is now unconscious.* The script form of

---

* These life scripts are plans, or programmes, imbedded in the Child ego state in early years. They can be winning scripts projecting a pattern of health, resourcefulness, progress, happiness and success, or losing scripts projecting a pattern of insecurity, illness, failure, suffering, early death and even suicide.

communication was essentially 'Don't be angry', or 'Be a good obedient girl, and mother will love you', or 'Children should be seen and not heard', or something like 'Honour thy father and thy mother'. I do not think the Commandments really mean that open confrontation to or genuine resentment of parents implies disrespect. In fact, I believe that true respect in any relationship is shown by direct expression of your authentic self even if that expression involves your anger. At this point, to cope more effectively with your hostility, you need to make a decision — a decision to re-programme your personality, to accept and tolerate your hostility for the purpose of resolving your daily problems.

In the present, in the Here and Now arena, if you look at people who cry, you realize that some of them are really crying with anger. Helping them to become aware of their 'cry anger' allows them to use it in an adaptive way.

Justified anger

Can you only accept anger if it is justified or reasonable? In other words, must your hostility meet your standards of conscience (Parent ego state) and rules of logical thinking (Adult ego state)? Actually, most angers are based on the angry Child within us, on the principles of irrationality and magic. If you can only accept the justified, logical and reasonable anger, then you are most certainly going to have to mask and deny a lot of your hostility.

A young girl, recently rejected by a boyfriend, went into a state of depression. As she cried in the therapy session, I asked her to imagine her boyfriend in the 'empty chair' and to talk to him in the here and now. She yelled out, with tears, 'You liar!' As she heard her angry Child yelling, she said, 'I have no right to be angry.' However, she did have an angry Child that was hurt and enraged by the rejection. Accepting the angry Child within herself and even ventilating it, in fantasy, brought some relief from the sadness. Some of us have to learn that angry Children do not have to be justified.

'Is the anger I see just me?'

or

'I'm not mad, he is!'

One night, a friend and I were engaged in an exciting and emotionally stimulating argument. All of a sudden, he grabbed me by the shirt, shook me and yelled at the top of his voice, 'You're so angry!' At that particular moment, the only hostility he could see was the anger he was projecting on me. He was totally unaware of the rage and hostility within himself. Frequently we deny our own anger by projecting it on to other people. In a sense it is a form of 'mind-fucking',* whereby we handle our own hostility by denying and avoiding it and pretending it only exists in other people. We can really play 'games' with this technique, because once we say that other people are angry we can justify our own resentment of them and then go around feeling 'I'm OK, you're not OK', being suspicious, mistrustful and resentful of others. An extreme form of projection is, of course, full paranoia. One example was a sick farmer who felt that the police were after him. He took out his shotgun and shot at them as they drove past his farm. They shot back, which proved his point.

The technique of projection has far-reaching social, cultural, national and even international effects. By disowning our aggressions, angers and hates – our 'badness' – and projecting these unacceptable traits on others, we produce prejudice and racism. Once we have labelled and scapegoated others as 'bad', we can then justify our resentments, cruelty and hostility towards them.

'I'm so upset!'

How often do you say you are upset? You usually mean that you are anxious, tense and uncomfortable. However, when the 'upset' feelings are explored, I often find an emotion of anger. I often discover resentments in people who think their own hostility is unacceptable.

I once had such an experience at the local 'Y'. I was sitting with another psychiatrist when a rabbi came in and joined the

* See page 127.

conversation, which concerned the State of Israel. He told of the difficulties he had raising money, and then with increasing fervour and loudness condemned certain wealthy citizens who were not contributing enough to the cause. Near the end of the discourse, he yelled, 'I am so upset with these people!' At this point my colleague quietly interjected, 'You mean angry,' and the rabbi, as if making a remarkable discovery, stated, 'Yes, I am really angry.' This was as effective a piece of psychotherapy as I have ever seen, and it took only about five seconds in the steam-room.

'Hurt' is another word often inappropriately used, especially by women. A woman I know kept feeling 'hurt' in various situations: hurt by her mother, hurt by her husband, hurt by her friends. She finally recognized that it was her anger, expressed it, and cured her 'hurt'.

Acting-out

Some people suppress their hostility and, without realizing what they are doing, act it out in their behaviour. A young married man began to steal and to have sex with prostitutes. He seemed to be driven by a strong impulse, and yet he felt his behaviour was wrong. In a session with him and his wife, I found the following relationship. The wife, while attempting to speak from her Adult, or logical, ego state, spoke to her husband like a critical mother, even shaking her domineering index finger at him. He, though trying to respond from his Adult ego state, sensed the sneaky smile of his mischievous Child, who was out to get her. As he got in touch with his anger and became aware of it, he began to ventilate it openly and directly to her. Whenever she treated him like a bad little boy, he talked back verbally. Before long he and his wife were fighting more openly with words, and his destructive behaviour disappeared. Surprisingly, they received an additional reward, for as they fought each other more they also loved each other more, and their sex life improved tremendously.

The automobile is one of the commonest devices people employ for acting out their hostility. Cutting off other drivers, passing recklessly and driving at high speeds are common ways of acting out hostility. No statistics are available, but I wonder how many automobile 'accidents' are really suicides – the acting-out of suppressed, self-destructive anger.

Shy

How often have you talked about someone you know who is quiet, withdrawn and passive, and said, 'He is very shy'? While a lot of so-called shy people may be apathetic, withdrawn, frightened of rejection and bored, and appear to be the opposite of aggressive, they are really passive-aggressive. I mean that the passivity or withdrawal you see can in itself be an indirect expression of hostility. It is like a sit-down strike – very, very passive, but intensely defiant. People who sit silently are often rebelling against giving any part of themselves. In group therapy, for example, silent people frequently tell you how frightened they are to speak up, and yet deep down they are saying, 'Damn you, I'm not going to talk and give you any part of myself.' It is like a soldier saluting his superior officer with his thumb sticking up his nose, or a sky writer going in behind a cloud and writing 'nuts'. Shyness and passivity can be an extremely powerful weapon of hostility. It is difficult to cope with and, unfortunately, does not allow for any resolution of problems. The one who suffers most of all is the passive person himself.

Zombie talk

A university professor of philosophy and his depressed wife, Natalie, had a combined IQ double that of most couples. They were aware of a severe marital conflict as well as of the wife's intense depressive illness. They could not communicate. They had the right words, yet they had almost completely suppressed and hidden their feelings. They said words to each other that may have been correct but were almost meaningless. They could not love, fight or cry. When they were asked what they felt, they usually replied with a thought, a concrete fact, or some attempt at explanation. Their feelings were dampened and blunted. Without feelings they could not use their superior Adult reasoning in any appropriate problem-solving way. They were both suffering from emotional deadness. They were 'zombies'.

Zombies are 'all head and no guts'. They speak without feeling, frequently in a monotone. They talk clinically, intellectually, and often play the game of Let's Analyse, or 'Play Psychiatry'. One woman, who hid her emotions almost completely, actually remembers her mother as being overactive and hysterical. This woman also recalls making a decision at one time that she would not react like her mother. In most human relationships she hides her emotions.

Some people can even talk about their anger but do not express the appropriate feeling that goes with it. Unfortunately, even though they have intellectual awareness, they are not allowing themselves personal gratification through emotional expression. Some people can even be bubbly and emotional; yet, when it comes to anger itself, the message goes through their heads, 'You just have to get a grip on yourself' or 'Peace at all costs'.

At any rate, Natalie suffered intense feelings of depression and anxiety. She required tranquillizers and anti-depressants to keep her partially comfortable. Occasionally she had outbursts of violent rage, in which she would pick up a knife and go for her husband or herself. Natalie could not make any progress in psychotherapy even though intellectually she knew what was going on. All of her feelings were suppressed and then they either spilled out in the form of anxiety or depression or burst forth in temper tantrums or explosions. Natalie had decided to hide her feelings because they were too painful, and it seemed to her that avoidance was the only way to look for comfort. Recovery for Natalie could have been simple. All she really had to do was to face her emotional discomfort, allow her words and her voice to express her feelings from moment to moment, effectively use the combination of feeling and thinking, and so come to terms with a discordant marriage.

Many of us feel that showing our feelings is a weakness or indicates loss of control. So we often praise 'keeping cool' or hiding our emotions. Zombie talk is an almost total suppression of feeling, and the most completely suppressed emotion is probably hostility. Unfortunately, many people, in order to hide their rage, suppress the whole alive, feeling Child ego state.

Jealousy

Jealousy has many faces: the sadness of losing someone you love or something you want, the anger towards the successful rival or over the loss itself, the feelings of low self-esteem and self-blame – essentially, self-criticism for the loss. Jealousy can reach unbelievable extremes, even resulting in murder.

A jealous lover's anger, especially, knows no bounds. One enraged man, following the break-up of his engagement, abducted his former fiancée. He took her to the edge of a cliff, put a rope around her neck, and dangled her over the edge. Fortunately, as she cried out, he came to his senses, pulled her up and took her to a hospital.

During group therapy, one young woman was surprised as she recognized her jealousy towards the other women in the group. She recognized jealousy whenever I, as the therapist, gave attention to other females. She then looked back to the first act, the beginning of her jealousy, when she was the middle and neglected child in her family. She was able to feel her sadness and anger towards the past as well as the present 'rejection'. Another woman was so jealous of any attention paid to others in the group that she slouched, pouted and silently withdrew. While her body movements expressed the anger of jealousy, she was only aware of feelings of sadness.

Jealousy can be prominent in any depressions where the illness, with its low self-esteem, produces feelings of envy towards people who are seen in a desirable position. As most people come to terms with their 'not OK-ness', and as their self-esteem rises, their jealousy decreases.

Sick with anger

There is a whole area of physical distress and psychosomatic illness directly related to hostility. I think that anger turned in – suppressed or released internally – is probably one of the most important factors in this type of physical illness. I also find that the anger is often combined with a hidden problem revolving around dependency-needs, which will be discussed later under the heading 'Me too'. People who have psychosomatic illnesses have usually repressed most of their hostility and have little or no awareness of its existence. They exhibit what might be called an 'ostrich syndrome', with their heads buried in the sand, when it comes to being in touch with, or having awareness of, their feelings, especially those concerned with hostility and de-pendency. The illnesses I see vary tremendously; they include arthritis, fluid retention, weight loss, obesity, fatigue, repeated upper respiratory infections and asthma. The stomach is a prominent area for 'eating yourself up', resulting in gastric upsets and attacks of diarrhoea or constipation, some of which lead to duodenal ulcers and colitis. Hypertension and heart disease fre-quently have a strong emotional component, and I also find these common in people with repressed hostility. Migraine and headaches of all sorts are common complaints of psychiatric patients. Low-back pain is another ailment that often seems to indicate considerable locked-up hostility. Finally, the skin is a good reflector of anger, and many dermatoses are psychoso-matic. Breaking out in hives is probably one of the most common ways in which the skin screams with rage.

'I will be mad at him for the rest of my life!'
or
Holding a grudge

Holding on to old resentments can be very painful, yet it is an extremely common habit. It is the Child in us that attempts to gain some end, or justify a way of life, by holding on to barrels full of hostility.

One man whose wife had committed suicide a number of years earlier was still suffering from a depression that began at her death. Through exploration in therapy, we found under-neath the man's depression an intense anger at his wife for killing herself. He was holding on to old rage. I asked him to talk to his wife, here and now, by imagining her in the 'empty chair'. As his hostility burst forth, he recognized that his anger was an attempt to manipulate his dead wife. Talking to his wife, as she sat in the magical 'empty chair', he yelled, 'I'll be mad at you till you come back and look after your children!' By venting his rage, then forgiving her, her behaviour and her suicide, and giving up the impossible plea for her return, he finally completed his mourning process and carried on with today's living, depression-free.

Another example of this was a fifty-year-old man who suffered from depression and migraine headaches and had a personality style that could be described as overly nice. In therapy we began to open up intense resentments to his father, anger that he could remember since he was four or five years old. His father had been dead for about eleven years, but still he hung on to his resentments. What for? Until when? When his anger was explored, the patient's magical Child said, 'I'll be mad at you, Father, till you really love me.' This was an expectation and a demand that had never been fulfilled when the patient was a small boy, and surely never could be fulfilled, since he was now a grown man and his father dead. The patient for many years had clung to tons of hostility that he could not handle effectively and that he only turned upon himself, in the production of headaches and recurrent depressive illnesses.

Scapegoating

In a group setting, Ronda accused Mary of seducing her boyfriend. Mary exploded with a kind of screaming rage that was both excessive and inappropriate. As she expressed her anger, she began to recognize that she was really ventilating twenty years of rage – rage that really was aimed at her mother, who had constantly preached that 'sex is dirty'. Mary remembered her mother scrubbing her vagina as a child and saying how dirty this area was. Mary scapegoated me with her rage throughout the therapy, for she saw me as representing different aspects of her parents.

How often do we express our anger in the wrong place, at the wrong time and in the wrong amount? Children especially are easy to scapegoat, for they quickly hook our angry Child or critical Parent. It is easier to scream at children than to face our wrath towards adults. A young man I know summed up scape-goating by saying, 'I take out my anger on the people closest to me.'

'Don't get close!'

Many people use their anger as a way of avoiding closeness or intimacy. Eric Berne described one example, the game of 'Uproar', in which father and teen-age daughter continually fight in order to avoid any closeness that might risk incestual feelings. What better way to avoid warm feelings than by fighting ? Closeness is sensed by many people as being dangerous because it entails risks. If you allow yourself to get close, you might be rejected or get hurt. You might even destroy people by your closeness and affection. If you get close, you may have to indulge in some sexual behaviour, and that may frighten you. When you get close to other people, you may become dependent on them, and perhaps you cannot trust any form of dependency – not even to admit that you have dependency needs. You may be concerned about revealing yourself to be inadequate, inferior or stupid. So if closeness is dangerous to you, keeping an angry distance between you and other people can be your means of defence against the imagined dangers of intimate relationships.

A married woman who was continually becoming enraged at her husband kept bursting forth with statements like 'I won't let him touch me.' She related an incident from a number of years earlier, when she had been severely depressed and was hospitalized. During a weekend visit at home, her husband had demanded sex. This had so infuriated her that she had held on to her resentments ever since, in order to prevent any recurrence of loving and sexual behaviour between the two of them. As she said: 'Doctor, what can I do with my intense hostility ?' Of course, the risk was to give it up, but then she might have to test out loving relationships again with her husband.

Flight or fight

In any crisis or threatening situation, you get ready to flee or fight. The aggressive drive to fight is accompanied by a surge of adrenalin, a constriction of your blood vessels, the rapid beating of your heart, the tightening of your muscles, and intense feelings of aggression and hostility towards the attacker or the threat. Your hostility and aggression are necessary for survival. Whenever you are under stress, nervous or scared, your anger will be present and will be expressed in your behaviour.

Most people understand and accept their anxiety and hostility under obvious stresses, but I wonder how many of us recognize our angry feelings in more subtle situations. Do you recognize how angry you are when somebody infringes upon your territory? Just walk down a busy street and see people's angry reactions as you infringe upon their path. Even in group therapy, people often seem to stake out their own territorial limits, by always using a particular chair as their security. We resent intrusions upon our psychological territory – strangers coming into the group, for example. There may be nothing wrong with the stranger; but just the fact that he is an intruder may cause us to react to him with a hostility that we usually deny ourselves in social situations. The stranger to the group likewise resents the others, who have such a firm holding in the social setting.

People also get angry when they are sick, hungry or tired. How often have you been aware of coming home from the office grumpy and irritable, and then finding that your feelings are relieved by a good meal? Literally, feeding the hungry Child soothes the savage beast.

3 The boiler of anger

Rage attacks, temper tantrums, violence and any excessive blowups of anger are mainly due to excessive controls or repressions of hostility. In other words, people who really cannot express their hostility in a direct and genuine way from moment to moment are the ones most likely to be subject to angry explosions. I call it the 'boiler theory'. Can you imagine the mind as a boiler filled with layer after layer of hostility and without adequate release valves ? As the boiler fills, a little extra pressure or some minor incident may trigger the explosion: an explosion of rage that is disproportionate to the incident. I have frequently seen this principle operate in individuals and I am sure that it also holds true in social problems of rioting and revolution. The greater the controls and the repression of hostility, the greater the risk of rage explosions and violence.

'Blowing your top' can be a vicious circle. People who find their anger unacceptable repress it, but then the boiler fills and explodes. The explosions seem to confirm the dangers of the anger, so it is suppressed even further, which produces a continuous cycle of rage attacks. The prevention of violence and rage attacks thus has two aspects: the reducing of anger production, and the learning of techniques of expression that prevent build-ups.

Tom is a veteran who since the war has suffered severe periods of depression, has made suicide attempts and has undergone recurrent and prolonged periods of hospitalization. Even today, he is disabled emotionally and unable to follow his career in art, for which he has real talent.

During the war, he was in the midst of battle and saw killing, brutality and violence; but, more important, he became aware of his ability to kill without hesitation. As a platoon leader, he felt responsible for sending his colleagues and friends to their deaths while he survived the war. He still feels guilt over having survived, as well as guilt over his potential for violence and killing. He is so fearful that his rage will erupt and explode that he is constantly on sentry duty to suppress it. Nevertheless, he has periodic outbursts of rage during which he physically hurts people he loves, or attempts suicide. These outbursts usually occur when he is under the influence of alcohol.

His horror of violence is often symbolized by 'flashbacks' to the war. Seeing someone eating, for example, brings back the picture of a young boy he shot. The boy was eating at the time and food and blood spilled from his mouth. Tom has been pensioned off as a result of his war neurosis. He firmly believes that his rage is excessive and murderous in character. He has geared his whole life to the problem of keeping his anger under control, but periodically it erupts. These rage explosions only confirm his fears, and he attempts to suppress his anger even further.

Tom is avoiding his angry Child, and in order to do so, he often suppresses the whole feeling aspect of his personality and comes across as an emotionless, mask-like person. He has very poor techniques for expressing his irritation 'here and now', from moment to moment.

Can he 'go to' his anger instead of suppressing it? Can he change his approach to his own angry Child ego state? Can he allow his anger to emerge, so that it can be used creatively and adaptively? Will he take a chance again and let out his angry Child, instead of repressing it and then going from repression to angry explosion?

The battered child syndrome
The medical profession has become aware in recent years of what is sometimes called the battered child syndrome. A young child or infant is viciously beaten by a parent. The child is taken to the hospital, where X-rays reveal old multiple fractures, suggesting that there have been repeated beatings. Surprisingly, the parents I have seen in such cases are often quiet, emotionally blunted, passive people who handle most of their irritations by repression and avoidance. Of course, the boiler fills; and a cranky infant may trigger an explosion of violence.

Too much hostility
How much anger is normal? How much is excessive? There are people who always seem angry and ready to explode. In

some cases, it is a brain abnormality that causes the excess of hostility. Then there is the criminal-psychopath, who channels his anger into violence and directs his hostility against society. He often comes into contact with the law, but rarely seeks psychiatric help. Because I am a private psychiatrist, I see little criminal behaviour. Most of the extremes of hostility that I see are of a verbal and psychological kind, and I would like to discuss them by reflecting again on the Child, Adult and Parent ego states.

'Give it to me !'

Many adults have an excessively demanding Child. Without their being aware of it, this Child is yelling, 'Give it to me!' It is continually making demands on other people, and when these demands are not met it responds with anger. Many of us still have this excessively demanding Child, even though it is beyond our consciousness. However, the over-production of rage from the frustrations of the Child's needs may burst through in a disguised way. Obviously, the greater the dependency-needs, the greater the hostility. The demanding Child beyond your awareness contaminates or disrupts your Adult. You think you are speaking logically, and you are unaware of your Child screaming in a disguised way, 'Give it to me!'

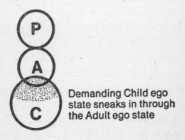

Demanding Child ego state sneaks in through the Adult ego state

'You are always picking on me !'

Excess hostility can also build up as a result of misinterpretation in our communication with people. Some of us tend to respond to others from the Child ego state. We mistake an Adult speaking to us for a critical Parent, and feel attacked. So we get angry in return. When we behave in this way, we are usually immature, hysterical and over-reactive. We are not aware that we are in the angry Child ego state. It is very important to listen to other people and to make sure that we clearly understand our 'transactions' (basic units of communication) with them. They may not be talking down to us or criticizing us; they may be giving straight Adult information.

Frequently, in group therapy sessions, I become aware of some words of a patient, or a particular body posture, which I want to explore further. As I approach the patient, he may react to me as if I had attacked him and respond with a remark like 'Get off my back,' or 'You're always picking on me.' His angry Child misinterprets my approach and responds as if I were a critical Parent. He could have avoided the over-production of anger by asking for clarification of my message.

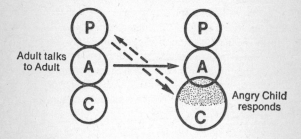

Adult talks to Adult

Angry Child responds

Too many shoulds

Excessive anger is often produced by a person who has a perfectionistic, driving personality. Such a person has a big, critical angry Parent, demanding that he and you live up to his unrealistic expectations. He is full of 'shoulds'. His mannerisms provide indications of his authoritarian attitude. His anger is really excessive when the Child in him or other people fails his demands. Once he lowers his expectations, his anger decreases. To do this he has to get in touch with, and experience, his Parent ego state. He is usually not in the least aware that his

Parent is turned on, and thinks that he is in a purely Adult, logical role. However, once he is able to hear the unrealistic demand of his Parent within him, he may be able to control and reduce his expectations. Of course, he might have to deal with some old script messages that say 'Perform and you will be loved' or 'Work hard.' With the awareness and the experiencing of his Parent ego state, the perfectionist can lower his expectations and reduce his anger.

The critical Parent is bigger than the other ego states in the perfectionistic personality and is the dominant one; it also con-

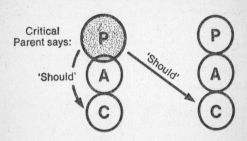

taminates the Adult ego state. In other words, the Parent ego state sneaks in, or disrupts, the Adult. Frequently when a person thinks he is in his logical, reasonable Adult role, he is not aware that his authoritarian, tyrannical Parent has crept in to rule his and your Child ego state.

Alcohol and drugs

Alcohol and many psychedelic drugs blur the ego states. First the Parent controls relax, next the Adult computer goes, and finally the Child ego is exposed. Frequently the Child's feelings are anger; a boiler of rage that has been suppressed explodes. Many alcoholics, when sober, totally deny their hostility, only to become violent when intoxicated.

One alcoholic patient, during a group session, trembled with intense anxiety. He described his feeling as 'the kind a great big Bloody Mary would dissolve quickly.' I asked him to stay with his anxiety and feel it as much as possible. He began to feel it in

his hands, clenching and unclenching his fists quite spontaneously. He recalled his boxing days and gently threw punches
into the air. I asked him to punch some cushions, and after a
few punches his tension dropped. When I asked him to make
his punches vigorous, he suddenly opened up in an intense rage.
He felt murderous rage and his anxiety shot up. He then spoke
of his fears of violence and told us how he always attempted to
suppress his anger totally and to 'be a nice guy'.

The price of this suppression was anxiety and a desire for
alcohol. Hard work and participation in competitive games
appeared to give him relief from his tension, but only temporarily. As the group sessions continued, he recognized that
'speaking up' was for him a more effective and less threatening
mechanism. His anxiety in the group decreased and he explored
the depths of his anger on the level of feeling as well as on an
intellectual level.

4 Angry games people play

A game is really a kind of hidden communication that takes place within the individual and between people. It is a sequence of communications, or transactions, that appear on the surface as Adult-to-Adult exchanges of information but also have a concealed meaning that is beyond the individual's or the participants' awareness. Games of the sort I am referring to were originally described by Eric Berne in his book *Games People Play*. I would like to discuss with you a number of these games to show how they can be games of hostility.

'Kick Me'

'Kick Me' is a game that occurs within a patient's personality. It is called an intra-psychic game, meaning that it takes place internally. The Parent ego state is constantly 'kicking', criticizing or condemning the Child ego state. On observing the Kick Me player, you find that he utters self-derogatory remarks and makes self-critical gestures. These show that he is torturing himself. The Kick Me player is saying to the Child within him, 'I don't like you. I am angry at you.' He is turning his anger in upon himself.

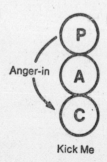

Kick Me

The Kick Me player is really out to get negative forms of recognition that he has been conditioned from early childhood to expect from his parents. He kicks himself in order to get some form of loving that he was used to receiving when he was younger.

In relationships with other people, the Kick Me player usually sends out messages that are as plain as if he were wearing a

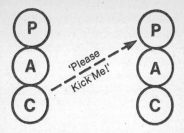

sweat shirt that says 'Please kick me'; and often people *do* respond, *do* kick him – and he gets his negative 'stroking'.

Lyn, a married woman with children, is an hysterical person – immature, emotionally unstable and explosive, excessively demanding, self-centred and seductive. Her Child ego state is fully exposed in all its splendour. She moves spontaneously from Child to Parent and back to Child without much Adult ego in between. Lyn is also a Kick Me artist of outstanding ability. Whenever her angry Child comes out, she brings in her critical Parent to kick it. Frequently she criticizes others, looking for rejection in return. If the rejection fails to materialize, she just kicks herself again for being so critical. She is getting attention almost continuously, either from without or from within, but always in the form of unpleasantness (negative stroking).

In groups or social situations, the Kick Me player often

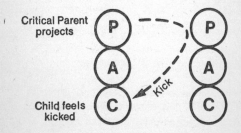

imagines that other people have Parents as critical as his, and he feels strongly that these other Parents in the group are criticizing or condemning him. This, of course, makes him feel anxious, uncomfortable and rejected.

'Now I've Got You, You Son of a Bitch!'

If two Kick Me players get married or decide to live together, they may play a game that Eric Berne described as NIGYSOB – 'Now I've Got You, You Son of a Bitch'. In this game the Parent of each party is out to get the Child of the other. For example, one of the two says, 'You are a lousy cook,' and the other responds with, 'You are a lousy lover,' and they go on attacking each other with no continuity of subject, solely for the purpose of ventilating hostility. While this is a terrible, conflictive sort of relationship, many couples, if they were to give up this game, would have nothing left. After all, if they stop fighting they may have to start loving, and many of us are extremely uncomfortable in the art of loving and closeness, and I do not mean just sex.

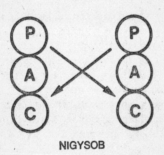

NIGYSOB

A NIGYSOB player and a Kick Me player create many variations of angry games and form a harmonious working arrangement in which they give each other angry, negative strokes. The NIGYSOB player, full of anger, might use a mistake that the Kick Me player has made as a rationalization for venting his hostility. The Kick Me player sees some logic in the NIGYSOB player's arguments and, overwhelmed by his own psychological need for kicks, accepts the negative strokes without fighting back. Since the NIGYSOB player is usually a Kick Me player as well, and vice versa, these two can easily exchange roles and spend hours in the pursuit of negative stroking through the ventilation of their anger.

You must be wondering what is wrong with NIGYSOB, considering that I have said all along that expressing your hostility is a good thing. The point is that, while anger can be problem-solving and self-abolishing, NIGYSOB involves continually blowing your top – blowing off steam with no other purpose than to 'get the bastard'. Some couples play NIGYSOB in a hidden way. Part of the remedial treatment is to help them to play it in an open way – to see it, hear it, feel it and then stop it.

In one case that I treated, a wife complained that her husband was unbearable to live with, often having temper tantrums. As I sat in the first interview, I noticed that the wife was out to get him. Every time she accused him of some kind of misbehaviour, he tried to handle it by a logical response. For example, when she blamed him for being cheap and stingy, he tried to give a logical explanation about his money and finances. She then switched to criticizing him for hitting the children. When he attempted to look objectively at his behaviour with his children, she criticized him for not completely finishing some repairs in the house. And so on. Now, in this game, the communication was crossed. The wife was trying from her critical Parent role to get at her husband's Child, while he was attempting to speak from his Adult to her Adult. They really were not communicating at all, and a very unpleasant thing was happening: the

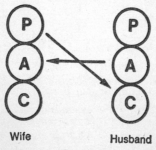

Wife   Husband

husband was denying how angry his Child felt towards his wife: he was trying to use this Adult logic to hide his angry Child, and while this worked for short periods he would eventually fill with rage and explode, according to the 'boiler theory', because he had not ventilated his hostility.

The solution was quite simple. From moment to moment when his wife played NIGYSOB, the husband could respond directly with his angry feelings and stop her onslaught of Parental criticism. With awareness, his wife could also recognize her angry game and switch, hopefully, to an Adult role.

Keep it cool
This is another variation of a marriage fight in which, for example, the woman vents her angry complaints while the man tries to 'keep it cool'. He operates on the motto of 'appease – peace at any price', and tries to ignore her and to play down her angry feelings, sometimes withdrawing in silence. This form of communication only further enrages the wife, and leaves conflicts unresolved.

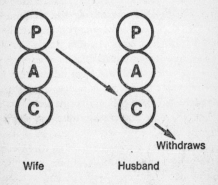

Withdraws

Wife   Husband

The angry games go round and round
The combinations and permutations of the angry games people play are infinite. Continuous angry interactions can become circular, with bickering and arguments that lead nowhere. A married man in his fifties had periods of impulsive behaviour in which he frequently ran away from home to strange cities

where he went on sex binges, viewing all the pornographic exhibits he could find and indulging heavily in sex with prostitutes. At home he was a peaceful, respectable, sexually impotent man. His wife, on the other hand, was a proficient NIGYSOB player, who performed dramatically with hysterical outbursts of crying, shaking, cursing and blaming. The more she screamed, the more he withdrew from the fights, and the more frequent his trips were. Their neurotic form of fighting had persisted for years until the marriage began to break up and they sought psychiatric treatment. The most surprising fact was that they had not recognized that his episodes of promiscuity were an acting-out of his rage towards his wife. Now both of them are in the process of learning to fight open, fair and straight.

Manipulation

Manipulation is the conscious playing of a game: getting at somebody by way of the back door. It is a wheeling-dealing, conning type of communication – a purposely devious effort to influence someone's behaviour; for example, consciously using a suicide attempt to get attention or to express anger. A young woman I know had sexual intercourse with a stranger simply in order to be able to tell a girlfriend, who in turn would inform the young woman's boyfriend. In this way she would get revenge for his running around with other women.

It is amazing how a person will manipulate or attempt to control another person's behaviour 'for the other's good'. Some women, for example, pretend to have orgasm during intercourse, when, in fact, they are not feeling much at all. I know of a mother who secretly spiked her twenty-year-old son's coffee with amphetamines, to make him alert so that he could study more effectively for his university examinations.

Any kind of manipulation, to me, is an angry gesture, even if it is for the other person's 'benefit'. People think that in the fields of psychology and psychiatry we therapists make people better by manipulating them. Maybe we do; but, if so, it is beyond my awareness, for true manipulation is deceit.

5 Sex and hostility

Impotence

A man who always spoke with great pride of his sexual powers failed one night to get an erection. This was the beginning of a period of impotence that coincided with a state of deep depression. As we explored his problem, he began to reveal an accumulation of hidden resentments. Some weeks later, at home, he had an open, angry encounter with his wife. His hostility exploded and burst outwards towards her. Much to his surprise, after his anger had been released, his penis began to work again. After the fight he made love as well as he ever had in the past.

Another man, a passive-aggressive personality, handled his aggression and hostility by evasive, stubborn and silent means. In his marriage he was totally impotent. His wife reacted with intense and open hostility, resenting not only the lack of intercourse but also the resulting lack of children in her home. After a number of weeks of treatment, he admitted that he was able to have intercourse with women, but only outside marriage. He was still sexually impotent with his wife. His impotence was one of the devious and indirect ways in which he dealt with hostility in his marriage.

The conscience, in Transactional Analysis terms, is the working of the Parent ego state, and it may inflict anger on the Child ego state by what has been described as a Kick Me process. I have seen a strange expression of the conscience in married men who have adopted the new sexual freedom of our time. They apparently feel guilt-free concerning extramarital affairs. However, even if 'all systems are go', the penis refuses to function in a strange bedroom; it is as if the change in conscience has been effective everywhere except in the shaft of the penis.

A common cause of periodic impotence is a depressive illness. While the loss of sexual drive is probably on a physiological basis, it is interesting to note that a good many depressions are really unresolved internalized anger. One man summed up his problem of impotence quite simply by stating that he was actually 'screwing my wife by not screwing her'. As he became aware that he was acting out his hostility through sex, he regained his potency.

Frigidity

Many of the frigid women I have seen, especially the married ones, are really mad as hell. Usually the anger is directed at their husbands. Their frigidity and anger are almost completely conscious, as they continue to rebuff their husbands' advances or respond from duty alone. Of course, some of these women are mad because they are not getting much pleasure out of sex. It is surprising how little some couples know about sexual techniques, even in our enlightened times. They fail to realize that many women only climax through direct stimulation of the clitoris, usually manually, and that this is perfectly normal. You do not really have to 'climax together'. Women's climaxing through intercourse alone, I find, is generally infrequent and restricted to 'the lucky few'.

Exhibitionism

During acute anxiety attacks, a young man in his early thirties would get an intense impulse to expose his penis to women. This action would not only relieve the anxiety but give him a sense of pleasure and excitement. He would not have come for treatment except that he was charged under the law for exhibitionism, and this motivated him to look for help. The mental examination revealed him to be a very pleasant, soft-spoken young man who was submissive and felt that raising his voice was indecent – so he raised his penis instead. We only had a few short visits and then he told me that he suddenly began to speak up for himself and to be more aggressive, and that he was feeling much less anxious. He also stated that with the disappearance of the anxiety he no longer had the impulse to exhibit himself.

'Rapo'

Eric Berne described 'Rapo' as a game with a superficial message of flirtatiousness. In this game, a woman usually made advances towards a man and led him on to great expectations. However, while the tease was great and the promise was good, the pay-off never came. The indignation the man felt at being denied his final sexual pleasure gave the woman satisfaction. The message of the game, deep down, was anger towards men, yet it was covered in a cloak of sexuality. Most of the women I tell this story to feel that men are just as guilty as women of using this game.

Masturbation

The hostility in masturbation is usually in the form of a Kick Me, or a turning of the rage in upon oneself. It is amazing that, of all sexual encounters possible, masturbation remains one of the most difficult for people to accept. Even today, when we know that there is no harm from masturbation and that it is perfectly normal behaviour, many people suffer intense pangs of remorse and feelings of inadequacy about it. Strangely enough, today, with greater sexual permissiveness, more people feel more sexually inadequate and incompetent when they self-indulge. They usually berate themselves severely for this normal behaviour.

A married man was depressed and, in spite of adequate sex in his marriage, he continued to masturbate frequently. The self-punishment, or guilt, produced a self-blaming depression. After discussing the masturbation with me, he agreed to accept it. In other words, getting his critical conscience off his back was sufficient to relieve his depression. As he was able to accept his masturbation, he was able to talk openly with his wife, and they were able to clear the air and resolve some of their communication difficulties and marital problems. While the couple's sex life did improve somewhat, and the man masturbated less often, he still continued to do it. But now he was able to accept it as part of his normal living, and functioned without any emotional impairment.

At a later date this man recognized that he masturbated to relieve anxiety and that under his anxiety was anger. As he dealt with his anger directly, his tension decreased and his desire to masturbate also declined.

Kick Me Sex

A certain woman indulged in sex, but not really for sexual pleasure, or even for attention or out of loneliness. She only wanted to prove that men are a 'bunch of bastards', that all they want is sex. She failed to realize that the attitude she held was an intense Kick Me, a denial of herself as an attractive personality—even a denial of herself as a desirable sex object.

Another young woman told me how her father had broken up her first serious romance and sent her to another city to forget her boyfriend. She began to date again, and on the first night was assaulted and literally raped. Surprisingly, even though this was her first sexual experience and an extremely painful one, she liked the young man and thought that if she dated him again his violent behaviour would not recur. She dated him a number of times and each time was painfully assaulted. Yet after each incident she felt that it would not happen again. Her behaviour illustrates an intense form of Kick Me sex. Essentially, it was a neurotic, self-destructive acting-out of suppressed rage towards her father.

Many men and women have a poor sexual identity, formed purely on the basis of their neurotic game of Kick Me. If you criticize and belittle yourself, then surely your self-concept in the sexual area suffers. You have feelings of sexual inadequacy. From this starting point, any sexual encounter will be filled with intense anxiety, fear of failure and rejection, and possibly impotence.

Homosexuality

I am puzzled as I look at homosexuality in terms of hostility. I feel that aggression is a problem in this area, yet I have not been able to observe it in clear-cut patterns. I think one reason for this is that many of the homosexuals I have seen have not been strongly motivated to change their sexual orientation. Many quit therapy after coming to terms with other aspects of their personality or neurotic problems.

The male homosexuals I have seen are not generally effeminate, yet seem to have a personality armour of pleasantness and softness. Homosexuality appears frequently as a denial or avoidance of hidden feelings of hostility. One young homosexual developed with me an angry-dependent relationship (see page 95). It appeared that his homosexuality was an acting-out of anger towards all men, originating with his father. We worked our way through an angry transference, in other words, the main therapy focused intensively on his relationship with me. As he began to relate to me from his Adult ego state, rather than as an angry Child, permitting us to talk on an Adult-to-Adult level, his periods of homosexuality decreased and he became heterosexual. In fact, as far as I am aware, he is happily married today.

Another homosexual man, in his early twenties, began to recognize that he had been a Kick Me specialist from his early years. One day he became conscious of some 'logical' (?) Child thoughts: 'I'm bad. Homosexuality is bad. I'm a homosexual.' His sexual identity was essentially a reflection of the psychological game of Kick Me, rather than a direct sexual inclination.

A young woman, after months of therapy, finally revealed that she was actively lesbian. As she said this, she noticed a surprised look on my face and burst out laughing. At that moment, she was aware of her angry mischievous Child, which had adopted homosexuality as a rebellion against traditional parental standards.

Another man with a self-destructive script was bisexual and would have periods of promiscuous homosexuality, during which he was occasionally beaten up physically. These flare-ups of homosexuality accompanied periods of self-blaming depression, during which his suicide script was running rampant. Making a commitment never to kill himself helped to decrease the periods of self-punitive behaviour, and he began to have more intense relationships with women as well as more emotionally genuine involvements with people in general.

Summing up, we can say that expressions of anger, hate and love often go together. Linguistically the word 'fuck' is probably the most hostile of words, yet it refers to the most intimate of sexual involvements. Most people who get angry flare up and direct their anger towards the people closest to them. Most murders are committed within a family or a love setting. The people you love and care for are the ones you respond to the fastest with hostility. When you are unable to express your anger, you usually have difficulty in feeling and expressing your love and sexuality as well. When you open up your hostility you may turn on your sex as well.

6 Body talk and anger

The body often speaks with a clear angry message while the mind is unaware of it. A professor of English became depressed shortly after the birth of his first child. As he described his state of depression, he shook his fist. Only his hand seemed to know how angry he was. When he got in touch with his hand, concentrated on the hand, talked for it and exaggerated its movement, he finally sensed his repressed hostility. As he openly acknowledged his feelings of rejection towards his newborn child and discussed it with his family and me, his depression lifted.

Watch the hands of people as they are talking and see how often a fighting gesture is made. You may be surprised how often the hand is clenched into a fist and the body movement reveals anger; you may also notice how often the shaking fist symbolizes the anger that is beyond the person's awareness. Repressed anger may cause people to have stomach distress, and such people often place a fist on their abdomen as they describe their distress. Some talk about the 'butterflies', or nervousness, in their 'gut', but only the fist seems to know about the rage within them.

Body posture often tells a story of aggression or readiness to fight. Many of the people I see in therapy sit in passive defiance, with stiff body and crossed arms and legs, cutting themselves off and keeping their distance from me. In states of extreme anxiety, people shake with marked tremors of the whole body. They are literally shaking with rage, each muscle tight and ready to fight. I have seen some angry women whose hostility only showed up in what I call the 'hostile hustle', a quick side-to-side swing of the hips. Clenched or grinding teeth frequently occur in angry people, even during sleep. I also recall an angry girl who blew cigarette smoke out through her nostrils like an angry bull, yet had no awareness of the intense rage she obviously felt.

The eyes speak volumes, ranging from affection to rejection: the opening of the eyelids with excitement and warmth, and the closing of the eyelids with coldness or withdrawal. I have been most impressed, in problems of communication, with the gaze. How difficult people find it just to look at each other! Depressed, suspicious, angry people frequently look away as they talk to you. It is strange how the gaze is associated with hostility. Somehow it is considered rude to stare at strangers.

The position of the feet and legs also can send all sorts of messages, from sexuality to aggression. I once had a patient, a volatile young lady, whose foot started to tap immediately when she was mad.

The loudness, tone and quality of the voice tell us much. How often the angry Child can be heard in the tone of voice, and yet the individual is unaware of his hostility! Frequently the words and the feeling expressed by the voice seem incongruous. Words of anger may come out while the emotional expression in the voice is restrained; a whining tone expresses clearly the demands, and the anger at the frustration of the demands.

Some people who hide their feelings have a mask-like face, almost expressionless. Their facial movements are minimal – they just barely move the lower jaw when they talk, and the remainder of the facial muscles remain immobile. Tense muscles of the jaw, neck and shoulders may suggest locked-in hostility. Often, through manipulation of these muscles, the anger can be brought into awareness.

We are all familiar with expressions such as 'stiff neck', 'seeing red', 'getting under my skin' and 'hair standing on end' that indicate hostility in body talk. I am totally amazed to observe how frequently the body seems aware of anger that the mind completely blocks. In Here and Now therapy I observe the body expressions in communications, to find ways of helping people experience their hostility.

3 The masks of anger

7 Depression

If you have ever been depressed, you will remember the extreme mental anguish and the intense emotional pain. Although the depression is totally involving, like a big black cloud, you may be able to differentiate the two main features of depression, which revolve around the two areas of thinking and feeling. The feelings are of intense sadness, gloom, pessimism and hopelessness. The ideas that seem to revolve around you continuously are of personal inadequacy, worthlessness, inferiority, failure and guilt. The depression may have followed the loss of someone or something you loved or even the loss of personal health. You may not even be aware of any real loss, or the loss may be impending. I think we all accept sadness as realistic and appropriate when we have lost something, but how many of us will recognize and accept the intense rage and indignation we feel at the loss itself?

I see mainly two kinds of depression:* a self-blaming depression and a claiming depression, which can occur separately or mixed with each other.

Claiming depression
In a pure, claiming depression, you feel inadequate and intensely helpless and alone. There is low self-evaluation, but usually little expressed self-criticism. The depression is a masked cry for love and attention. Like all of us, you need affection and stroking for recognition. However, you do not ask for it directly because you believe it is unacceptable to have these needs, so you do so symbolically through the cry of sadness. The hope is that some loving parent figure will come and rescue you from your unpleasantness. Your body may be bent, your lips droop, your head hangs low and your claim is for love.

One woman in a claiming depression recalled every unpleasant moment of her life. She knew the details and time of each upset and related them with clarity. Obviously, her Adult

* See Silvano Arieti, 'The Psychotherapeutic Approach to Depression', in *American Journal of Psychotherapy*, Vol. 16, July 1962, pp 397–406.

ego state thought that, if I knew every traumatic experience of her life, I could solve her problem. However, her Child ego state was really indulging in what I call 'graveyard digging': picking out every past unpleasantness so that she could feel badly and, in a sense, play the hidden game of 'Poor Me', or 'Ain't It Awful'. The game was really her Child's plea for loving support. As she unconsciously experienced the game of Poor Me, she was finally able to put away her past misfortunes and carry on with everyday living. When she needed affection and attention, she could go to her husband directly and ask for it.

A single girl decided to move out of her parents' home and into an apartment. At the time of the move, two boyfriends dropped her and she went into a claiming depression. In this depression, she began to feel and dress like a much younger girl. As the depression was explored, she experienced an intense feeling of loneliness and a strong desire for affection. Her lonely Child was hurting, but she attempted to hide this because she only wanted to admit to being grown up and independent. Once she accepted the emotional hunger within her, she was able to accept some help from her parents. She saw them frequently, spending some evenings with them, staying for dinner, in an attempt to gratify her loneliness until she was ready to step forward into the world. The gratification of her emotional hunger, through her parents, allowed for partial relief of the claiming depression.

In a claiming depression, when you cry for love and no one answers, you get angry in response to the frustration. You do not express the resentment directly or openly, however, for fear of missing a chance to receive affection. Your anger is then turned in as a self-blaming aspect of your claiming depression.

Kick Me depression
or
Self-blaming depression

A self-blaming depression is one in which you are continually blaming yourself for your misfortunes. You may recognize that you have not done anything wrong or harmful, yet you continue to play the game of self-torture, or Kick Me. It is a psychological game and by its very definition is unconscious, beyond awareness. You really do not know that you are kicking yourself. You are not aware that your Parent ego state is continually kicking, criticizing and tormenting the Child ego state within you.

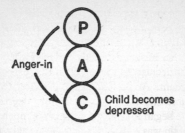

In a sense, what is happening is that within your personality you are turning all of your hostility and hatred upon yourself. As I said before, you are really not aware that you are doing this, even though you feel the intense repercussions of the behaviour, the intense pain of emotional sadness, and ideas of poor self-esteem. Frequently the anger you turn upon yourself is hostility that you actually feel towards others: anger that you will not express or even fantasize outwardly.

Now, while this game of Kick Me is unconscious, you can learn to tune in or listen to yourself on a level of experience, and hear your critical Parent ego state saying things like 'You are stupid,' 'You failed,' 'You're inadequate,' and other self-derogatory remarks. For example, one patient kept saying to himself, 'What the hell is the matter with you?' Another woman kept hearing herself yelling at the Child within her, saying, 'Stupid, stupid, stupid.' Sometimes she would say, 'Why, why, why? Why am I depressed?' This, while it sounded like a logical search for an answer, was usually the voice of a critical and castigating Parent saying, 'Why are you so depressed, when you don't have any right to be that way?' Another woman would frequently look in a mirror at herself and yell, 'I hate you!'

I have heard many patients in a self-blaming depression say,

49

'The trouble with me is that I feel sorry for myself.' Such patients feel that they cause their depression by being excessively sympathetic with their own problems, and of course nothing could be further from the truth. For when you listen to the tone of their voice, you can easily hear self-directed anger and blame, not sympathy.

A depressed young woman, a college teacher of English, spoke with a clear diction and a free flow of words. At times, however, when she thought she was in her Adult ego state, giving information, the group began to detect a Jewish accent and to notice some dramatic body movements and gestures. They pointed this out to her and soon she was able to hear within herself the voice of her critical Jewish mother. After that she was in touch with her critical Parent ego state, which had been continually kicking her and had produced her depressive illness, and was able to use her Adult to control it.

Many people dwell on past mistakes and failures in a self-critical way without the awareness that they are playing a neurotic game of Kick Me. Sometimes the 'kick' in depression is experienced through the words of the Child ego state itself. You may then be aware of such 'I' feelings as 'I'm no good,' 'I'm ugly,' 'I'm inferior,' 'I don't deserve anything,' 'I'm nothing,' 'I'm garbage,' 'I don't deserve to live,' 'I'm scared of everything,' and 'I'm a failure.'

Double or triple Kick Me

Some people in a self-blaming depression not only kick themselves but continue to do so in a vicious, circular manner. A woman I saw recently, having kicked herself for being angry during a party, got depressed. She then kicked herself for being depressed, because she felt she should not be so weak. The depression continued and she came to me for help. Again she kicked herself, this time for requiring professional attention. Some people live with a bunch of 'should nots'. Continuing to play Kick Me in this vicious circle only aggravates and increases the feeling of depression. This particular patient returned for a meeting some time later and told me that she had not told her husband that she was going to consult a psychiatrist. After the initial meeting she told him; but even though he was pleased that she had sought help, she felt ashamed for telling him. Again, another circular Kick Me.

Let me put it to you in the form of a mental picture. Imagine someone hitting himself on the head with a hammer, while not aware of what he is doing, and walking into a doctor's office saying, 'Doctor, my head hurts.' The doctor replies, 'Of course. You are hitting yourself on the head with a hammer.' The patient then says, 'Ah,' and recognizes that he is inflicting his own suffering. The next question he may ask the doctor is, 'What do I do now?' and of course the obvious reply is, 'How about stopping it?' It is amazing how the hurts of depression stop when you halt the self-torturing game of Kick Me.

In most psychiatric descriptions of depression, authorities say that the mood of sadness comes first and the depressive, self-critical thinking follows. However, since becoming involved with the concepts of Parent, Adult and Child, I am most impressed with the idea that the self-criticism is primary and the mood follows. Of course, once started, it is a repetitive, vicious circle. Psychiatrists have seen the mood of sadness as the most obvious. Yet I have watched this mood change quickly, as the critical Parent comes and goes within the individual. The patient who comes to a psychiatrist is usually aware that his unpleasant feelings of depression are there, whereas the Kick Me game is usually beyond his awareness. The trick, of course, is to get in touch with the Kick Me game and then stop it.

One example of a Kick Me depression was a teen-ager in his final year at high school who became seriously depressed, with subsequent deterioration of his school work. He used his school difficulties to prove to himself how stupid and inadequate he was. He blamed himself for not doing his work, and for not keeping up with social and other interests. Not only did he continually criticize himself for his failure to do well in school but he felt guilty for letting his father down. He was sad and had withdrawn from most of life's activities. Even in group therapy he sat quietly with his head hung low, and, when asked what he was experiencing, would state how terrible he was for sitting there and not participating, for 'just feeling sorry for himself'. He thought that other people in the group were criticizing him for his behaviour. This young man was actually turning in upon himself his natural rebellious feeling for emancipation. He subdued his rage towards a controlling and domineering father, turned the hostility upon himself and produced a self-blaming depression. As he improved, he began to externalize many of his aggressive feelings. They occasionally burst forth in some sexual behaviour and he sometimes got drunk. As he began to direct his aggressiveness towards the external world, his depression decreased. Finally, with time, he was able to express his irritation openly and directly, and the acting-out of his aggression subsided. He became assertive and was able to stand up to his parents. At this point the father called my office. He complained that his previously quiet and obedient son had somehow become an angry, loud and rebellious demon in the home. No, the young man was not depressed any longer; but certainly he was creating new problems – both for himself and for his family – as he ventilated his anger outwards into his environment.

Another case of self-blaming depression occurred in the director of a large public institution. He developed intense feelings of inadequacy and felt totally unable to handle the job that he had been doing satisfactorily for many years. The only thing we could learn was that, at this time, the pressures within his job were intense and there were many complaints and dissatisfactions among the staff. With his increasing tension and frustration, the director found himself unable to function. The symptoms were so painful that every time he entered the door of the building he was flooded with intense panic and feelings of gloom. Many times he retreated back to his home and bed. He would often sit in my office telling me how inadequate and incapable he was and suggesting that he should retire from his job and give it to a more capable person. However, as he began to turn his anger outwards where it belonged, he began to rebel against the pressures of business and of the staff, and, as he spoke out instead of in, his depression lifted and his self-confidence returned. Today he is continuing successfully at his job.

Sometimes awareness itself, even on a level of experience, is not sufficient to stop the self-punishing game. You may have a life script that could be called a 'loser' script, in which you use the game of Kick Me to perpetuate a basic life-style of suffering or self-destruction.

For example, a shy, withdrawn, emotionally cold young woman had a loser script buried in her Child ego state at a very early age. This script said, 'Closeness and intimacy are dangerous.' Without being aware of it, she designed her life to avoid closeness with others. As she grew older, closeness also meant the risk of sexuality. The possibility of sexual involvement frightened her and strengthened her script which said, 'Don't be close.' In order to maintain this life-style, she developed the almost continuous process of Kick Me in all important relationships and in all major areas of her life. The constant barrage of self-criticism and self-ridicule led to intense depressive illnesses, which resulted in her withdrawal from people important to her and enabled her to maintain her basic life plan of avoiding intimacy. In order to stop the self-punishing game, she would have to change her life script to something like 'It's OK to be close.'

Are you guilty?

A concentration-camp survivor still suffers intense guilt over having survived. He feels so guilty that unconsciously he has sentenced himself to a life of suffering and unhappiness. When

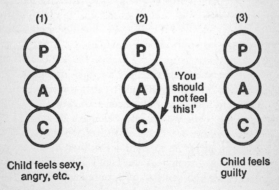

(1)   (2)   (3)

'You should not feel this!'

Child feels sexy, angry, etc.

Child feels guilty

he recently had a pleasurable and exciting sexual encounter with a beautiful woman, it was followed by an intense attack of anxiety. He saw me for emergency consultation and we explored the panic. Just under the surface was the old guilt, ever-present and extracting its payment of suffering for any experience of pleasure.

Whenever the Child within us experiences any feelings – from sexiness to frigidity, anger to sadness, nervousness to fear – that the Parent ego state finds unacceptable, then the Child reacts with feelings of guilt. These feelings are essentially the result of the Parent's criticism and rejection of the Child's feelings.

Ninety per cent of guilt is anger. The anger you turn upon yourself in feeling guilty, if dealt with objectively, would be resentment of others. Most depressions involve some feelings of guilt: feelings of wrongdoing, of failing to live up to expectations, or of letting friends or parents down. When you really explore the guilt, get in touch with it, feel it, and experience it,

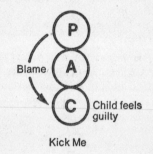

Kick Me

you may recognize it for what it is: a mask of hostility. When you really look at guilt, you see that it is a form of Kick Me, with the Parent blaming the Child for wrongdoings.

A mother, a social worker, came to me with intense feelings of guilt and sadness over her teen-age son's delinquency, which involved drug-taking and a jail sentence for possession and peddling of drugs. Frankly, if she could have felt and expressed her anger at her son over his behaviour, instead of masking it, this would have been more effective and constructive than turning the anger upon herself in the form of a guilty depression.

The 'Guilty' game can be more complex. Some people, when they feel anger and will not express it outwardly, turn it against

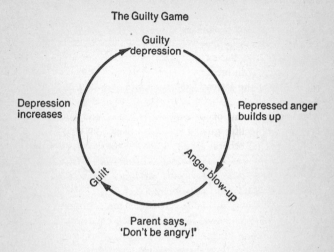

The Guilty Game

Guilty depression

Depression increases

Repressed anger builds up

Guilt

Anger blow-up

Parent says, 'Don't be angry!'

themselves and feel guilty. Occasionally the anger rises to such intensity that it bursts out towards others and becomes almost a rage attack. These people then feel guilty about having expressed unjustified and irrational hostility and become more depressed. It can be a vicious circle of guilt: blowing up with anger, then feeling guilty over the anger, and so becoming more depressed. At some point in the Guilty game the Kick Me must stop for recovery to take place.

Shame

Shame, disgrace, embarrassment and humiliation are all critical Parent words. Like guilt, shame may be a form of internalized anger, excessive or inappropriate – that is, on a neurotic level.

One patient of mine, a married woman, had a strange love affair with a married man. The two would make love, and then he would withdraw with guilt for a period of weeks, leaving her alone and unhappy. She was desperately in love but she was filled with shame. She felt like a prostitute, 'screwing behind my husband's back' and 'totally responsible for my lover's discomfort and guilt'. Her shame was condemnation by her sense of morality; but deep down she was angry with her lover. She was angry over his periodic rejections of her, his withdrawals and vacillations. Yet she found it intolerable to experience the anger for fear of losing his love.

Kick Me behaviour

I have described how people feel and think in a Kick Me or self-blaming depression. Some people, rather than experiencing their depression purely in terms of feelings and ideas, act out their depressive illness in behaviour – behaviour that in itself is self-destructive. For example, much criminal behaviour is depressive acting-out. A crime may be committed in such a way that obvious clues are left, leading to quick apprehension of the criminal, so that society actually inflicts the kick.

A young woman in her late twenties could probably write a book about her self-destructive, Kick Me behaviour. Once she took an old car in for repairs at one of the best garages in town. The bill was more than the whole car was worth. She then condemned herself for poor judgement and felt depressed. Another time, in an affair with a married man, she recognized that she disliked him; nevertheless, she continued to sleep with him, and felt ashamed of her behaviour. There were many other examples of her self-destructive behaviour, ranging from auto accidents to abuse of drugs. She was amazed as she became aware of the Kick Me. She recognized that much of her behaviour was primarily for the pay-off of sadness, pain and suffering. She also recognized that she was heading for a final pay-off, or life plan, of suicide. She made a decision to live and quite quickly stopped her self-destructive behaviour. She even began to come up with creative ideas and new pursuits.

I am continually impressed that so many women use sexual encounters as part of a Kick Me process. It is as if they pick a man who will seduce them, then hurt them and leave them. As they become aware of themselves through therapy, they see that they have been setting up the whole pattern of painful inter-action and rejection.

Many people who act out their depressions may not be aware that they are depressed. Effective psychotherapy therefore be-comes painful, and they must experience the emotional dis-comfort of their depression before they can resolve it.

'What am I worth?'

It is not easy to put a price on your own head. From a chemical point of view, you are probably not worth more than a dollar or two, which would hardly be worth the cost of extraction. For your ability to work, you can be paid on a normal scale, and there is a schedule of fees for almost every kind of occupation or service. But what are you worth just as a human being? This is difficult to measure, yet each of us has some sense of self-value. In almost every situation, we are weighing our assets and liabilities.

Dr Thomas Harris, in his book *I'm OK – You're OK*, gives us some useful measuring guides. If I'm OK and you're OK, then I get on with living and am emotionally healthy and fairly stable and happy. If I'm not OK and you're OK, then I am usually depressed, with low self-esteem, and mainly concerned with getting away from life and people. If I'm OK, but you are not OK, then I am suspicious, distrustful and looking for ways of getting rid of you. If I'm not OK, and you're not OK, then I am getting nowhere, except maybe going crazy. Dr Harris did not say it, but I have found out that, if I feel that I'm OK, then most people react to me as if I am OK.

Your feelings of self-worth and self-esteem are expressions of your Child ego state and depend on two things: first, the posi-tive signs of recognition or stroking that you get from the out-side world, your environment, and second, the positive signs you get from the internal world within your personality from the stroking you give yourself. Recognition from the outside world can be from your friends or from achievements in your work. The internal forms of recognition come from the Parent ego state, which, as we have seen, may be nurturing or critical. If your Parent is loving and nurturing, it will give you positive

57

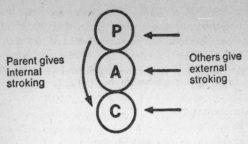

Self-esteem regulation

forms of love and affection, just because you exist, rather than only when you perform. Hopefully, the positive forms of love and affection that you get from within make you feel OK.

Depression, as we have seen, occurs when the Parent ego state kicks you, when your self-image is poor and you feel inadequate, inferior and guilty. Your mental processes of thinking and concentration are slowed down by the depression and this only adds to your poor concept of yourself. You may be successful or talented in work and still fail to realize that your low self-

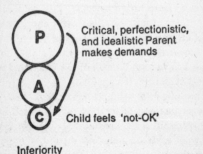

Inferiority

esteem is generated from internal criticism. When you listen to yourself again, you can always hear the critical Parent berating the Child and producing the unfavourable self-opinion. Even people who are not receiving much satisfaction or pleasure

58

from their environment usually have increased feelings of self-worth when they stop the internal game of self-criticism, even if their accomplishments in the outside world remain unchanged.

This can be summarized simply. If the nurturing Parent within you loves you and attends you and praises you, your feelings of self-worth will go up, and this is accompanied by feelings of well-being and pleasure. When the Parent ego state within you is critical and condemning, and demands that you live up to high, unrealistic standards, then your self-opinion is low and you feel sad and depressed.

The body beautiful

A poor body-image is another expression of Kick Me. You would never believe how many attractive people feel that their bodies are ugly. Their self-criticism is reflected in their observation of their physical appearance. Obesity is a common illusion: many people who are actually slender hate their 'fatness' and are preoccupied with unnecessary dieting. Many a woman with a poor body-image will consult a plastic surgeon to have her nose reshaped, her face lifted, or her breasts filled, when what she really requires is the removal of a critical Parent ego state. In depression, the body-image suffers along with self-confidence, and this is another expression of the Kick Me game.

How to stay inferior

First step, 'kick' yourself really well; for extra good measure add frequent 'gallows laughs' of self-ridicule, and you will feel inferior and dependent.

Next step, encourage others to belittle you. When you come into a social situation feeling like a helpless Child, you will hook the Parent in others. They will see your frightened Child and will respond to you from their authority role, which will only confirm your inadequacy. In a sense, when you show people quite quickly your dependent, shy position, someone will come to rescue you by playing good mother. The way others relate to you serves to emphasize your dependency and inferiority.

For example, a young man I know kept expressing his low self-esteem by the way he dressed. His shirts were dirty and torn, his shoes were worn and his general appearance was sloppy and dirty. He had a feeling about himself of 'not OK', and other people responded to him with criticism and rejection.

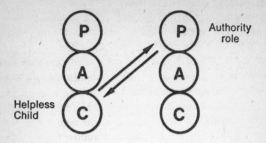

Swollen head

Giving ourselves positive strokes by saying 'I'm great,' or 'I'm beautiful' or 'What a nice guy I am' is something we frequently label negatively, regarding it as a sign of a swollen head. Somehow, positive stroking of ourselves has become shameful, unacceptable, conceited and indecent. In our early cultural development we stress being humble and modest. I am amazed at how we learn to view our strengths as something that we don't talk about. Why not? I think it is great to recognize and accept our humanness, our individuality and our assets; but we rarely do.

There are many cultural and religious taboos against positive stroking. For example, if a Jewish grandmother is out with her grandchild and somebody happens to say 'What a beautiful baby,' the grandmother then performs certain cultural rituals, like 'knocking on wood', spitting three times on the back of her hand or muttering the incantation, '*Kine eyen harah*', which means 'no evil eye', to ward off possible harm from the compliment.* It is amazing that many cultures of the past have held that positive stroking was capable of producing misfortune, and conversely, that suffering or unhappiness ensured a good life to come. We have learned to discount the art of positive stroking, especially positive stroking of ourselves.

* Mrs Helen Coulton, 'Knock on Wood', *Transactional Analysis Journal* 1:3, January 1972.

The Silent Tantrum
The following little chant occurs in children's folklore:

Nobody likes me,
Everybody hates me!
Think I'll go eat worms.

Nobody knows how I survive
On worms three times a day.*

The stance of the sulker, or pouter, is quite obvious in a small child. The child who sulks or pouts knows he is angry; but the adult who sulks usually feels depressed. His facial expression is a frown or scowl, but he isn't aware of the rage and hostility he is holding within himself. I sometimes wonder whether a sulker, if he could look objectively into a mirror and see his furrowed brow, the tense muscles of his jaw, and the grinding of his teeth, might not recognize his hidden anger and perhaps be able to deal with it himself in a direct and realistic way.

One man, during a group session, asked for a chance to discuss his problem, and began to describe it. When he was interrupted by another patient, who took the floor, he sat back quietly, closed his eyes, hung his head low and put his hand on his forehead. He sat like this for ten or fifteen minutes. His behaviour was obvious to everyone: the silent sulk or temper tantrum, and a plea for attention. Asked how he felt, he replied, 'Sad and bored.' But eventually he was able to feel his resentment at being ignored, and then he expressed his irritation openly and insisted on being heard, and on getting some attention for his problem. This effective use of his hostility removed his depressive sulk.

Anger-in or anger-out
Turning your anger upon yourself produces self-blaming depression. I believe that, if you get angry, you only have two choices of action. You can turn it on yourself, in some sort of self-torture; or you turn it out into the environment, even if this just means experiencing or fantasizing the hostility outwardly.

* From Edith Fowke, *Sally Go Round the Sun* (Toronto: McClelland and Stewart Ltd, 1969), p 94.

An example from the animal world may serve to illustrate the concept of 'anger-in or anger-out'. Experimenting with young monkeys, Dr Harry Harlow observed that, when they left their mother's side, they usually engaged in various kinds of aggressive hostile behaviour with other monkeys, including teasing and fighting. He observed that the monkeys were running around in a very excited way. But if a monkey at this age was isolated from its peer group, it actually went into a depressive withdrawal and began to tear at its own skin. This animal experiment demonstrates quite clearly that if the aggressive drive, of which I consider hostility to be a large part, does not come out it goes inwards in a self-destructive way.

Anger-out in the form of protest, rioting, violence and guerrilla warfare in Northern Ireland, for example, has brought with it a marked drop in depressive illnesses and suicides among the combatants. Every country involved in World War Two showed a significant decrease in suicide rates. This social evidence, published by Dr H. A. Lyons, an Irish psychiatrist, in the *British Medical Journal*, confirms my opinion that anger-out is a way of reducing depressive illnesses. Of course, I am not suggesting that we use violence to cure depression, but I do think that it is important to recognize that externalizing anger in socially constructive ways can cure depression.

I have seen many patients within a group setting get angry and either turn the anger upon themselves, resulting in an almost instantaneous depression, or be stimulated into turning it outwards, bringing immediate relief of the depressive symptoms and a feeling of well-being. The turning in of your aggression and anger leads to much more than depression; it leads to social withdrawal. Opening up your aggressive feelings and 'going to' your anger leads to social involvement, interaction with others, and the potential for intimacy and stroking.

Unfortunately, sometimes experiential awareness of the Kick Me game is not sufficient to stop depression. Terry, a single woman in her early twenties, had suffered years of recurring depressions. Her mother had a serious schizophrenic illness that persisted throughout Terry's life. When Terry was young, each time she got angry her mother would run downstairs and hide in the cellar. Terry eventually believed that her anger made her mother sick, and the Child within her made a decision never to be angry. Now, as a woman, Terry would not release her anger, which produced self-blaming depressions.

The turning in upon yourself of anger may become part of your life-style. Some people have a losing life script from early childhood, which says something like 'Suffering builds character,' or 'If I suffer enough I will be rescued, loved and protected.' This concept of martyrdom flows freely through religious and cultural beliefs. It really is not true, but unfortunately the Child ego state believes in magic. The script may be 'self-destruction' and the Kick Me may be the means of accomplishing the final pay-off, death.

Pleasure out of suffering

Many of us smile and laugh as we relate unpleasant things about ourselves. Sometimes this smile indicates the pleasure we receive from our own discomfort. This masochism may be a conditioner from early childhood, acquired from parents who stroked or recognized a child only when he was hurt or uncomfortable. This form of negative recognition of children is probably one of the most common reasons why some children grow up needing painful forms of attention in order to live.

We all need emotional food, just as we need physical food. We can receive many kinds of feedings. We can be loved simply because we exist. We can be loved by a parent only when we perform. But no attention or affection at all results in a situation of emotional starvation and is intolerable.

Some years ago, Dr René Spitz investigated a strange problem in young infants who were institutionalized. He found that these young infants, despite having their physical needs met with food and toilet care, began to become apathetic, depressed and physically ill. The condition seemed to be without physical cause; yet, when it persisted, some of the infants died. Upon examining the institution, Dr Spitz found that the nurses attending the children, although capable, were cold, distant and without emotional warmth. Simply by replacing these efficient but emotionally frigid women with warm, mothering types who

63

could give love, caressing and strokes, this 'anaclitic depression'* subsided and the children recovered.

Since the absence of stroking is intolerable, children settle for negative forms of recognition. They get attention for misbehaviour, sickness and suffering. It is better to be kicked than not recognized at all.

Unfortunately, these moulds of behaviour for getting emotional nourishment or stroking continue into adult life. As a result, such adults play games with unpleasant emotional pay-offs and turn the anger and hostility in upon themselves. In a sense, they are so conditioned from childhood to being criticized and rejected that they do the same thing to themselves by allowing the Parent ego state to berate the Child within them. A kick is better than being ignored. Would it not be great (although maybe it is unrealistic), in raising children, to love them for just existing and to avoid completely criticisms for misbehaviour? Many of us loving parents would be shocked if we could listen to a tape of ourselves and hear how negatively we respond to our children, and how much attention and criticism we give for misbehaviour.

I think it is OK, in raising children, to express any resentment of them openly from moment to moment as we feel it. We can use our critical Parent to control our children's aggressive and primitive behaviour and to set limits for them. I think it is also very important to recognize children and to share with them our positive feelings of affection. Most of the time, we simply ignore them – unless they are getting into some sort of mischief, and then we negatively stroke them, thereby conditioning them to receiving pleasure out of suffering.

The 'gallows laugh'

Who said it was great to laugh at yourself? We all do it, and we frequently encourage others to laugh at our mistakes. If you tune in to some of the laughter at your distress, you will again find the critical Parent poking fun at the hurt Child, or the Child laughing at its self-destructive behaviour. One depressed

* See René A. Spitz, 'Anaclitic Depression', *Psychoanalytic Study of the Child*, 2:313–42, 1946.

girl laughed at herself as she described her pain, her difficulties with school and her family problems. As she tuned in on her 'gallows laugh', she heard the voice of the belittling Parent. Remember, if you laugh at yourself often enough, you will experience pain – with some degree of emotional discomfort, anxiety or depression.

A depressed young man who had a tremendous sense of humour only used it on himself, during his depression, in a very belittling and critical way. He did this so engagingly that others frequently laughed at him and at his suffering. Essentially, he was poking fun at himself and encouraging others to laugh at his mistakes. As he began to direct his sense of humour out into the environment, he recovered from his depression and began to experience a real sense of pleasure and well-being from his sharp wit.

Suicide

Suicide can be the climax of intense feelings of self-hatred and the final pay-off for a Kick Me player. However, underneath many suicide gestures are expressions of anger towards people close by. A suicidal patient, when asked to have a fantasy about his death and funeral, will often imagine his close ones feeling guilty, and sorry that they did not treat him better. The patient may then recognize the pleasure he gets from revenge by imagining his close ones suffering over his death. One woman said to me, as she thought of her suicide, 'It will be on their heads.' I asked her why she needed a suicide attempt to express her anger, and why she did not just express it directly. She replied that if she told her loved one off he might reject her, whereas if she expressed the anger in a suicide gesture he might by some chance come closer to her (as a caring parent to a hurt child ?).

Suicide and murder appear to be closely related. Many patients have described how their violent suicide fantasies coincide and alternate with murderous impulses towards close relatives. One hysterical young woman could switch quite quickly from an attempt to kill herself to a violent attack on her husband. The intense anger exploded either in or out. Another depressed woman, as she indulged in her fantasy to kill herself during a group therapy session, found that she was moving into a fantasy about killing me, her psychiatrist. Surprisingly enough, this fantasy about murdering me brought intense relief from her depression and she enjoyed the ecstasy of anger breaking out. Many depressed people, when suicidal, feel that they have to take their children with them. They see the sense of hopelessness and suffering that surrounds them as enveloping the lives of their children too. Their own suicide and the murder of their children may seem, through the eyes of depression, to be the only way out.

Suicide is an extremely complicated subject. To some it can promise release from intense suffering; for others it can be a form of revenge for hurts suffered. For some it is a scream of rage and indignation. Some even hope that redemption will magically come through death and that they will finally be able to live with pleasure. Of course, this is not logical; but the Child ego state works on magic.

Good Kick Me players, who continually kick themselves, may be using this game to complete a life script that says 'Don't exist,' or 'Die.' However, I have seen people make a revision of their life plan, deciding never to kill themselves and to change their script. Following these revisions, I have been very impressed to note that many people do change their way of life. Since they are not going to die, they no longer need this terrible game of Kick Me. They no longer need to play the self-torturing game of 'anger-in'.

Mourning

The loss of a friend or loved one through death or separation may bring intense feelings of sadness and mourning that sometimes resemble a depressive illness. However, while the sadness is great, it is usually necessary for the cutting of the bonds between the living and the dead. We can always accept the sadness as natural and appropriate, but we usually deny the considerable resentment we feel about the loss of someone close. Basically and understandably, we probably feel anger towards the person lost for dying and leaving us all alone; sometimes the magical Child within us holds on to anger towards the loved one, as if to say, 'I will be mad at you till you come back to life.' We may even feel anger towards the world and towards God for the death. Or we may just feel anger at losing something that was important to us. However, these angers are often unacceptable to us and come out in a disguised manner. If they are turned in, we go through depression and anxiety. Often they go out, in which case we scapegoat people. For example, the physician who treats a terminal illness is often blamed for the death by the patient's relatives.

The feelings of hostility are frequently excessive if you are relatively dependent and helpless. But, surprisingly, it is easier to come to terms with the death of someone you loved than with the death of someone about whom you had mixed feelings. When you have had ambivalent feelings towards a person now dead, the mourning process is often prolonged and can lead to a depressive illness. Hostile feelings towards the dead are often unacceptable to the conscience of the living.

A young woman who had lost her mother seemed to come to terms satisfactorily with the mourning process, but remained depressed. She finally came to the basic awareness, on the level of experience, that she was angry at God for taking away her mother. When she expressed and ventilated her hostility, and gave it up, she was able to close the chapter on her mother and on her mother's death, and recovered from her depression.

It is almost unbelievable, but it does happen that excessive mourning that continues after a loss may be a way of keeping the loved one alive, emotionally. I recall a woman who stayed depressed for about five years after her husband's death. One day in therapy she described her home: there was her husband's chair in the living room, and there was his seat in the dining room, which no one had sat in since his death. It became so obvious to both of us then that she was not just keeping the memory of her husband alive. Rather, she was symbolically keeping her husband with her in the house. Letting him go, and letting him die within her, facilitated the end of her depression.

We frequently fail to recognize that there is a mourning process for separation as well as for death – a process by which we say goodbye. An attractive young actress was plagued by chronic depression after the break-up of her marriage. It was only after about two years of depression that she emotionally let go of her husband. The last step in ending the relationship seemed to be facing her hostility towards him, her resentments that she had kept hidden. These resentments she could not face at first, lest she endanger the possibility of his returning to her. Ventilating her anger cut the last string, and her depression lifted. She was then ready to get on with new relationships.

The rage at dying

People dying through sickness or ageing rarely seek psychiatric treatment to deal with the process of dying itself. Possibly in the future we will recognize that psychotherapy for the dying can in some cases be extremely important in helping a person come to terms with life in an effective and satisfying way.

Most of my contact with dying came during my experience as a general practitioner. It occurred to me that most people face their own deaths by emotional denial. An extreme example was a woman in her forties who was dying from secondary cancer. I sent her to a special hospital for radiation therapy. After she had had many treatments I saw her again in my office and she remarked to me, 'Doctor, you'd be surprised how many people are going to this hospital for radiation treatment for cancer.' At no time in the discussion did she recognize that she too was attending the clinic for that purpose.

Today, with our increased openness and our ability to confront people more directly, we are talking more frankly about the process of dying. While the dying person usually recognizes and experiences sadness over the impending loss of his life, he rarely faces his anger at death itself: death, the greatest insult to living man. Dylan Thomas expressed powerfully the feelings of anger and resentment towards dying in his poem 'Do Not Go Gentle into that Good Night'. He wrote:

Do not go gentle into that good night,
Old age should burn and rave at close of day;
Rage, rage against the dying of the light.*

* From *The Poems of Dylan Thomas*, ed. Daniel Jones (New York: New Directions, 1971).

Sadness and sickness

A woman, discussing her breast removal for cancer fifteen years previously, cried as she said, 'I have never felt like a woman since.' Her depression was still just under the surface. I wonder if she had ever ventilated her anger about the mutilation of her body. Whenever we become ill, there is some element of sadness. Although it appears acceptable to be low and to gain some sympathy when we are ill, few of us ever ventilate our anger towards the illness itself. Whenever you lose an important part or function of your body through illness, you will experience a mourning process over the loss, and this requires facing your anger.

Sad but not depressed

A depressed, suicidal woman faced her discordant marriage openly and recognized its deterioration. She then decided to separate from her husband. The separation became an open crisis for her child and created serious problems that made her sad. However, her previous feeling of depression, with its pessimism, hopelessness and low self-esteem, had disappeared. In other words, the depression had been an avoidance of the marital conflict. When she faced this problem directly, she became sad but no longer depressed.

How to respond to a depressed person

In responding to a depressed friend or relative, many of us are under the impression that because he is depressed he is weak, fragile and may fall apart – so, we had better be gentle. We frequently respond in a way that 'doesn't make waves'. We may offer him sympathy to help him avoid unpleasantness, handling him with kid gloves. Of course, this type of treatment only adds to his depression and to his feelings of inferiority.

I would like to suggest some better ways to handle a depressed person, primarily by using your ability to feel and think in the present. If you really use yourself openly and naturally in the present, with clear vision, as a young child might, you will see quite easily the anger in the self-blaming depression: the facial frown, the obvious sulk. By responding with your own sense of irritation, or in the way you feel towards the anger you see, you will produce interactions – maybe some explosive or hostile response that may help the depressed person come into contact with the feelings he is repressing. If he makes you angry, be angry. Have enough respect and concern for him to respond genuinely and directly. He will not fall apart. He is really not weak or inferior. He probably is quite a competent human being who is handling his anger in a pathological way. If the depression is primarily of the claiming sort, you will see the aloneness and sense of helplessness quite easily. Then respond as you do to a helpless child, but at least talk to him about it openly and directly. See whether his depression is a cry for love and affection. Maybe he can ask directly for recognition or stroking, without the mask of the claiming depression.

Above all, do not tell the person to stand up straight and tighten his belt. It does not help to show him that life is going really well for him, that he is much better off than the next person, that he has no right or reason to be depressed. He knows this, and this kind of argument will only make him feel more guilty about his depressed position. Use your feelings to reach him, for the psychodynamics of the depression operate on the level of the emotions.

Summary of depression

In all Kick Me depressions the Parent beats the Child unmercifully. If a real-life parent treated his children with such brutality, he would be tried, convicted and jailed for child-beating.

In a self-blaming depression, the constant barrage of self-criticism leaves the Child ego state feeling helpless and inadequate. Very low self-esteem leads to a claiming depression, with intense cries from the depressed person to anyone with whom he has an important relationship, especially with his psychiatrist. 'Please help me' is a desperate plea from a person who feels totally unable to cope. Thus, the self-blaming depression has gone in a circular direction to a claiming depression, and leads around and around from claiming to self-blaming with increasing depth of the depressive response. I find that, for many patients, the way to break this vicious circle of spiralling depression is to get in touch with the internalized anger and express it openly or even in fantasy. This frequently allows them to face stressful problems of life and to resolve the depressive illness.

Depressive illness is primarily an aggregation of physiological, behavioural and psychological symptoms. Your body responds with gastro-intestinal disturbances that range from nausea, to loss of appetite, to constipation, to abdominal pain. Your weight may fluctuate – up or (more frequently) down. Your sex drives decrease drastically and, in women, menstrual irregularities are common. Muscle aches may be disabling and your body may respond with intense fatigue. Insomnia may be severe; you may have difficulty in falling asleep, and find yourself fully awake in early hours of the morning. The days are painful, and the mornings frequently unbearable; sometimes by evening there is a drastic clicking off of unpleasantness and a return to feelings of well-being. Your whole psychological and physical system slows down, your thinking becomes dull, and your ability to concentrate lessens. Memory impairment and indecisiveness are common. You become intensely frightened and have periodic outbursts of crying. You are flooded with feelings of sadness combined with feelings of unworthiness and guilt. Or there may just be an emptiness that alternates with periods of anxiety and irritability. You seem totally preoccupied with your own distress and have difficulty in even thinking, let alone caring, about others. Suicidal ideas run rampant and periodically switch to fears of insanity.

The above description is a short summary of the primary experience of depression, but there is an aspect of depression that in psychiatric terms is often referred to as a 'secondary gain'. It can be summed up simply by saying that 'depression is anger'. The depressed person, totally involved in his own pain and distress, withdraws from people close to him. His friends and relatives may see his way of acting as a rejection of them. It is paradoxical, for in many cases the depression is a mask of anger and yet the depressive behaviour, in a secondary way, really expresses hostility towards others.

8 Anxiety

Anxiety attacks

Karen had been tense and nervous for most of her adult life. At times, panic occurred, and she choked and gasped for breath; yet there was nothing physically wrong. Her fears were meaningless and silly. She could not leave home alone without intense fear. Sometimes she would go out in the car and then become petrified after driving only a short distance, as if there was a big sign that read, 'Danger, don't go beyond this point.' Going to parties and any kind of socializing was frightening for her. She became intensely nervous and critically self-aware, and felt very inadequate. Her mind went blank; her speech became hesitant, with many slips of the tongue; and her words stumbled out, jumbled and mumbled. Her anxiety in the presence of company sometimes mounted to such an extent that she was afraid she might lose control, explode and go completely crazy. Sometimes this social anxiety was so intense at a party that she had to go home. One night, when Karen was walking downtown with her husband and another couple, they saw a street brawl. The fight was on the other side of the street, a safe distance away, but suddenly panic struck her; she turned, went out of control and ran away. She was aware that she could not stand fighting of any sort. She was aware that anger in any form, especially in herself, produced intense fears in her. She knew that her husband was sometimes overbearing, critical and domineering, but she could not speak up to him. After all, he might leave her if she protested, and she was afraid of being alone.

Anxiety is a state of extreme nervousness – disproportionate fear that sometimes reaches an unbearable pitch called 'panic'. Sometimes it is the first level of neurotic defence against emerging anger. Anxiety, while it can be very painful, is the healthiest of the neurotic responses in that it is the one closest to the basic disturbance. It is as if we were peeling an onion and anxiety were the last layer next to the core of angry feelings. Anxiety is acutely painful, almost unbearable, and, if prolonged, usually ends in depression.

Anxiety can be felt as emotional distress or, as often happens, as physical discomfort. There was a young woman who had serious attacks of chest and arm pain, rapid pulse and extreme anxiety. She had been checked medically many times, and knew there was no evidence of heart disease or any other physical disorder. She was very frightened, however, because several members of her family had died relatively young of heart disease, and she knew the hereditary significance of this. Her attacks occurred at the strangest 'times: in a social situation, in a heated discussion, during a telephone discussion with her mother-in-law, and, much to her surprise, even when she was entering the synagogue. As we worked through her phobias and her fear of sickness, we came to a basically angry woman – a woman who was angry at many things but who rarely expressed it. She was angry at her husband and angry at her mother-in-law, who always rejected her. She was even angry at God for taking away so many of her relatives at an early age. Facing these angers, accepting them, and then dissolving them led to considerable improvement, with marked relief from her anxiety attacks (her cardiac neurosis).

Phobia

A phobia is a specific unrealistic fear. It is a localized anxiety attack in a situation that is normally not dangerous or threatening, but to which the person reacts with extreme fear. Phobias are as varied as your imagination. They encompass fear of animals, fear of planes and cars, fear of closed spaces and open spaces, fear of crowded places and high places. Some people panic in an elevator while others are unable to face a flight of stairs. Many people are intensely frightened of sickness and some are preoccupied with a fear of dying.

Many respond with inappropriate anxiety to sex. For example, one young woman described to me her sexual phobia with her lover. While making love, as soon as they began the act of intercourse, she burst into an attack of phobic anxiety – a totally inappropriate response to her conscious desire for love.

The automobile can become a source of much anxiety. Some people are preoccupied with a fear of accidents, of unintentionally killing others or themselves. One woman had a fear that she would be shot while driving; this fear was a projection of her own aggressive impulses. Another patient was unable to drive his car without panic – and this was the only visible sign of his emotional illness. Some people, as they walk down the street, develop a fear that a car will somehow come off the road and kill them. Occasionally patients tell me of the phobic fantasy of whipping the car wheel around impulsively with the desire to drive a car at a high speed into an abutment. One patient's first awareness of his own emotional illness came while he was driving; an intense anxiety overtook him, and he recognized an almost unconscious desire to kill himself by colliding with a bus.

Phobias can be attached to almost any situation or person. One young woman was driven into intense panic by aloneness and troubled by neurotic fear of the dark; she frequently found herself too frightened to sleep. Phobias are masks and displacements of underlying problems, particularly sexual conflicts. In my practice I often find a phobia to be the mask that covers a core of anger, with the phobic symptoms totally displaced and unrelated to the sources of hostility. Sometimes the underlying problem is non-specific, a general suppression of aggression and hostility in important areas of life. As the person becomes more adept in assertion and defiance, he loses his neurotic symptoms of phobic anxiety.

Future anxiety – a phobia
Many people worry and remain very frightened about the future. They know as well as I that it is impossible to predict the future, but they continue to worry about it and fear it. In many of my patients with 'future anxiety' I find an excessive brooding, an obsessional type of thinking, which really controls repressed or hidden rage. Facing the rage and dealing with it appropriately usually diminishes the worrying about tomorrow.

One young woman who was often frightened about the future became acutely anxious in anticipation of her wedding. She was totally perplexed, for she was in love with her fiancé. There were no sexual, social or economic problems, yet she feared the future. As we worked in therapy, we uncovered a failure script in her Child ego state. From an early age, she had been given a hidden failure message by her parents, and her personality became geared to maintain this position. Her Parent ego state was continually saying 'It is not enough' to everything that she did. As her wedding day approached, her Parent kept belittling her status as a woman, and she felt inadequate for the role of wife.

Morning anxiety

One man said to me, 'I feel wrangy in the morning, on the days I have to go to work.' He usually awakened with a feeling of tenseness, irritability and nausea. Sometimes he would vomit and retch and he couldn't eat breakfast. In his anxiety, he was aware of fears – a fear of leaving home and a fear of being unable to make important decisions at work. Thoughts of work would spin around and around in his head, yet after he had worked for an hour or so, the tension would subside and he would feel comfortable. 'Why, why, why?' he would ask himself (the why's were really Kick Me's).

One day in the midst of his morning anxiety, he felt the grinding of his teeth and the clenching of his fists. As he vomited, he heard the voice of his angry Child yell, 'I hate this bloody job!' Then he realized his anxiety was a mask against unacceptable and threatening rage – anger that was dangerous because his work was his livelihood and he wouldn't give it up. However, his awareness and ventilation of his anger at least reduced the intensity of his morning anxiety. In depressions, morning anxiety can be intense and disabling, but at some time during the day it automatically clicks off, leaving the depressed person exhausted but relaxed.

Shaking with rage

Sometimes, as we experience our own anxiety, we may notice a tremor in our body, which may increase to an intense shaking. As we get in touch with the shakiness, concentrate on it, feel the tenseness of the muscles, even exaggerate it and shake more, we get in touch with some of the rage behind the shaking. If the rage is expressed and ventilated, our shaking subsides. While one young woman was telling me of an intense anxiety experience, her arms flapped up and down like wings until she recognized and ventilated her irritation about her husband.

Clicked out

Some people can mentally click out, the way you turn off a light. They can turn off their feelings and even their conscious awareness. We call it a 'disassociated state', an altered state of consciousness. One woman suddenly woke up and found she had a knife in her hand and was going to attack her husband with it. She had no awareness of what she was doing or why, and hardly any recollection of earlier events. All she knew was that she had awakened with the knife in her hand. Her anger was so unacceptable to her that she had to 'click out' the conscious awareness in order to act out unconsciously the rage she felt. Her old script message was 'You should get control of yourself,' which meant 'Don't be angry.' The only way she could really be angry was to 'click out'. Many of us click out emotionally – perhaps not as dramatically as this woman, but subtly and for short periods we turn off our feelings, our conscious state of awareness. The feeling we are repressing is our anxiety, and anger may be the next layer.

Some of us turn off our feelings and experience a state of emptiness or a blandness. To some, this state is a feeling of unreality or depersonalization. Some people click out of this life and click in to fantasies or daydreams. A young woman I know has the same two fantasies that she indulges in almost daily and usually withdraws into during periods of stress or tension. She sees herself either as a happy little girl with loving people around her, or as a mother with many lovely children living together in a happy home. She is aware that when she becomes frightened and anxious or fearful of rejection she withdraws into her serialized daydreams. More recently she has become aware that the frightened Child that runs and clicks out is basically angry and that essentially she is escaping from her hostility. As she visualizes anger she can only see it as a tantrum of hers as a young child in the past. Yet today she has a voice and the ability to verbalize resentments, whereas the old record of her as a young child with limited verbal capacity could only express rage in physical tantrums and screaming.

Social anxiety

I think most people are uncomfortable to some degree in social situations, and this is one of the reasons why alcohol, the fastest tranquillizer, is freely used. Social anxiety is like being alone in a crowd. We are surrounded by people, yet there is a sense of separation from the group; our basic need for real attention, and for affection or stroking, is being frustrated. If we do not get social recognition, the Child within us becomes angry. Our desire for attention is socially unacceptable. We hide it and as we push it down, as we try to suppress the Child's feeling within us, we experience social discomfort and nervousness. Notice how your anxiety level drops at a reception when someone approaches you and gives you some recognition or positive stroking. You may even enjoy the occasion, if your presence is recognized in a meaningful way. Even at private parties and gatherings of old friends, repeated transactions of recognition or stroking are necessary for re-acquaintance. If you are a self-torturer, a Kick Me player, you may use this social discomfort as justification to feel inadequate and to condemn yourself for being a misfit.

The Kick Me specialist is, of course, at a special kind of disadvantage when he enters a group situation. Already he feels inadequate and inferior because of his self-criticism. However, once in a social group, he immediately projects his critical Parent on to others and imagines that they are as critical of him as he is of himself. Ironically, he is not aware that most people are so busy trying to maintain their own self-esteem in social interactions that they are probably not evaluating him at all.

Often in a conversation we do not understand what is said to us, but rather than ask for clarification we pretend, by a smile or a nod of the head, that we know what is going on. Internally, we kick ourselves for being stupid. How much better it would be to stop at the point of confusion and ask for an explanation! Of course we could do this; but, since we are Kick Me artists, we do not do it, because we assume that it would be regarded as a sign of ignorance.

Calling yourself stupid, and imagining that other people are calling you stupid, results in a real scared Child who wants to withdraw from social contact and may even be panic-stricken at the thought of social encounters. By withdrawing, you miss one of the greatest pleasures and sources of recognition. Social-izing beyond your family circle is extremely important in grow-ing up. It helps you to emancipate yourself from the family bonds and to extend your life into the community.

Socializing can be therapeutic; it may even help to repair damage caused by inadequate parenting. Dr Harlow, in his animal behaviour experiments, separated a group of baby monkeys from their parents and fed them by cloth mothers (monkey dolls with a projecting feeding tube), thus depriving them of the emotional aspect of real mothering; they grew up to be damaged adult monkeys, as was demonstrated by their inability to perform sexually when fully grown. However, an-other group of monkeys, also separated from their parents and fed by cloth mothers, were given normal socializing through play with other monkeys; they grew into sexually normal adult monkeys. This is an exciting concept if we can apply it to human development. It suggests that children of inadequate parents can be 'repaired' or restored through good group relationships in school, play and work. Possibly one reason why group therapy seems so helpful and stimulating – regardless of the therapist's special approach – is that it offers an opportunity for socializing outside the family unit.

Hostility carried as a chip on the shoulder prevents closeness. Hostility turned inwards in the form of a Kick Me, and pro-jected as a criticism from others, produces an intense social anxiety that is often handled by social withdrawal. The combi-nation of the critical Parent ego state, the game of Kick Me and the resultant Child that feels 'not OK' produces an individual highly sensitive to rejection and finely tuned to any sign of neglect or withdrawal by others. The constant aura of rejection in any social relationship produces intense and chronic social anxiety.

The scared Kid

An anxiety state is really the scared Kid part of the Child ego state. A young man, during an argument in group therapy, responded with anxiety so intense that it persisted throughout the following week. On his next visit he told us how unbearable his anxiety had become and said that he felt it best to quit treatment. He did, however, agree to work on his fears during the meeting and attempted to get in touch with his frightened Kid. In the process, he began to feel like the small child of many years ago. He was being yelled at and beaten by his father and, as he acted this out, he kept yelling at his father, 'Please don't hit me.' Quite suddenly, he broke the psychodrama and told me off, and said he was going to intellectualize about his behaviour even if I did not like it. As he expressed his anger to the group and to me, his anxiety attack subsided. He recognized his intense resentment of me as the authority of the group and of his father, who had attacked him in the past. As he became more tranquil, he let us in on a revenge fantasy. Throughout the week, as he considered the idea of leaving the group, he had felt immense pleasure at the thought that he would be getting revenge on all of us.

Sometimes the scared Kid is a mask of anger and sometimes it is a genuine portrayal of a real situation. A young woman was faced all at once with several crises in her life. She had separated from her husband, had serious financial difficulties and was forced to return to work. Her new position of aloneness, and the need to face new responsibilities, produced marked anxiety. In my office, as she experienced her frightened Kid, she shouted, 'I'm scared,' and at that moment we both heard the self-criticism in her voice. She yelled 'I'm scared' in a self-belittling way; at the same time, she was really kicking herself for being frightened in her new world. This young woman would not accept or tolerate normal anxiety. Her self-criticism resulted in poor self-esteem, which only exaggerated the size of her scared Kid. Anxieties may be normal, and tolerating them without self-criticism prevents a vicious circle of increasing anxiety and depression.

Many of us face anxiety in preparing for special situations; Dr Perls called this 'stage fright'. When it is explored, the anxiety usually contains underlying expectations of catastrophe. The next time you are presented with some new stress, and you react with marked anxiety, sit back for a moment and fantasize on the catastrophes that might happen – perhaps you are afraid you will fail in the undertaking, or be rejected, criticized or laughed at. People might see your 'not OK' Kid. If you experience your old fears and concerns from the past, you may be able to bring in the Adult, here and now, to help you face the new encounter with less tension.

While anxiety may be a sickness, a neurosis or an acutely painful emotional symptom, nevertheless it may also simply be excitement. Frequently, anxiety accompanies new experiences. When you sense anxiety, stay with it, use it, live it and feel it, and you may then experience the accompanying sense of excitement and aliveness. Strange as it may seem, the pain of anxiety and the pleasure of excitement may be fused in the process of personality growth and change.

Agitated depression

Many people suffer from intense anxiety mixed or alternating with depression. This is one of the most painful combinations of emotional upset. The whole system is excessively active, tense with extreme restlessness, painful anxiety and agitated depression. This frantic depression stands out in contrast to the other forms of depression, which are apathetic and 'energyless'. I think that the mixture of anxiety and depression is really a boiler full of angry feelings, ready to burst. While the pain of the agitated depression is excruciating and the risks of suicide or homicide are high, nevertheless the crisis has the potential for quick resolution and personality growth, since it is very close to the underlying psychopathology of repressed rage.

9 The curse of perfectionism

The curse of protectionism

'Don't forget to put gas in the car tomorrow, dear,' Joe told his wife as he went to bed one night. In the morning, his wife found on the kitchen table a note from Joe saying, 'Remember to put gas in the car.' When she went out to the car there was another note under the windshield wiper: 'Remember, gas in the car, honey.' That night, she blew her top at Joe. She was angry and resented his repeated reminders. Joe could not understand her anger. After all, he was just being efficient and he did not want her to run out of gas. He was blind to his own personality style and quite unaware of his belittling behaviour. Joe suffered from the curse of perfectionism.

Are you a person who is excessively conscientious and serious, who works too hard and plays too little? Do you rely heavily on reason and pride yourself on intelligence? Do you demand perfection of yourself and expect high standards of the people close to you? Are you very competitive, ambitious and success-oriented? Are you extremely honest and idealistic? Is it important to you that you be neat, orderly, well organized, and punctual? If the above partially fits you, then you are no doubt praised as a dedicated, honest, hardworking and productive human being. You are probably even very successful and well known in your field of work.

However, if you display this kind of behaviour excessively, you are probably suffering from the curse of perfectionism. Those with this curse are inflexible and compulsive individuals who try to control others in a demanding, authoritarian way. People react with resentment to the perfectionist's driving nature and to his tendency to speech-making, preaching and over-analysis. He does not understand why people are irritated with him. He does not realize that his behaviour is hostile. He does not see that he is using logic and ethical constructs to mask his anger. He is using excessive 'shoulds', 'musts' and 'ought to's' to bring under control the angry, defiant Child that lies within him.

A young woman's perfectionistic personality had developed to such an extreme that she had to be hospitalized. Severe hand-washing compulsions were disrupting her life. She was constantly in the washroom, scrubbing her hands. She recognized that it was excessive, but suffered intense anxiety when she stopped the washing. Her life was plagued by periods of panic and tension. At one of our therapy sessions, she appeared in a highly seductive outfit, with most of her breasts protruding. Being a Here and Now therapist, I explored with her the meaning of the way she dressed for the appointment. Following my remarks, she released a flood of hostility and anger that had been locked up for many years. At the next few sessions, she berated me for being a 'dirty old man'. As her hostility came out week after week, she began to see that her rage was excessive and disproportionate to my questioning of her style of dress. And, as her hostility bloomed, her hand-washing decreased. The periods of anxiety were less frequent. She began to work and to enjoy life.

Another perfectionistic patient was at a professional hockey game one night when a fight broke out among the players. As the fight raged, the fans screamed, 'Get him, kill him!' The patient went into a severe anxiety state and felt like running out of the stadium. When the fight subsided, so did his anxiety. We worked this through in therapy and found that his anxiety was a shield against his own rage and hostility, which he controlled with his perfectionistic way of living. The open aggression at the hockey game had come close to opening the 'boiler' of angry feelings that he had hidden so well within himself.

Let's be logical

Your Adult computer, your use of reasoning and your intelligence are powerful personality tools that help you to adapt to the reality of life and the problems of living. However, rationalizing, making up excuses, over-analysing your behaviour and continually asking 'Why?' may be the over-use of your Adult computer for the purpose of avoiding the feeling that exists in you. One patient was rejected by our group whenever she spoke. She would go into a harangue, make speeches and try to play

'Let's Analyse' or 'Play Psychiatry'. She gave explanations for everything she did and explanations for the way others responded. The group reacted with irritation, for this person's sermonizing and rationalizing were phony. Actually, they were intense cover-ups for basic feelings of irritation towards the people around her.

Sometimes, however, under the disguise of logic, the critical Parent sneaks in with a word like 'Why?' The tone of voice indicates that it is not a process of reasoning, but rather a form of self-criticism. A word like 'but' in a seemingly logical sentence may come from the critical Parent and negate the entire statement. For example, a father may say to his son, 'It's OK to express your feelings, but don't talk back to me!'

Trifle expert

The perfectionistic, extremely logical person sometimes turns out to be an expert on trifles. Often he is overly talkative and rigid in his thinking. He may repeat the same idea to you over and over again, sometimes to the point of desperation. He deals with intricate details of any subject and over-analyses situations. He sometimes misses the tree because of his pre-occupation with the leaves.

A compulsive doctor in one of my groups would launch into some highly detailed thinking, concentrating on minute facts that seemed unrelated, whenever his anger was aroused during a group session. His tone of voice, as he imparted this rambling, factual information, was usually a monotone, devoid of any emotion. If his frustrations grew further, he would mentally start counting things, such as knobs on the furniture, people in the room or even holes in the ceiling tiles. As the sessions progressed and we helped him get in touch with his feelings, he began to express his resentments openly, and became emotionally alive. Once his hostility had been vented, he stopped his irrelevant fact-finding missions.

The 'trifle expert', in order to keep track of his many details, tends to keep lists. He usually has notes in his pocket of things to do and when to do them. He sometimes comes to the psychiatrist with lists of complaints or subjects to discuss. Little does he realize that these lists represent attempts to control his 'boiler' of angry feelings.

Indecision

It is amazing that the compulsive person, logical and usually quite bright, can be extremely indecisive. He may say repeatedly, as he looks at a problem, 'but on the other hand', or he may continually try to evaluate the pros and cons of an argument. This only results in his wandering from indecision to indecision. Indecisiveness can go to the extreme of driving not only the perfectionist himself but also the people around him crazy. The amazing thing is that the perfectionist is unaware that his indecisiveness is really phony logic employed to control his basic feeling of rage. If you ever see this type of person in a social situation, make a point of watching your irritation develop as a result of his indecision. If you watch him closely you may even see his smile of pleasure as he puts the other fellow down. Sometimes his arguments, presented under the guise of Adult logic and fairness, are really stubborn defiance. Frequently the perfectionist is in his authoritative Parent role and is playing Now I've Got You, You Son of a Bitch.

I think it is important to remember that, while you may be extremely irritated by the indecision of the compulsive person he himself is almost paralysed by the anxiety that accompanies his vacillations. He is quite aware that he has intelligence and the ability to solve problems, and yet he feels torn by intense feelings of insecurity and anxiety in making his decisions.

A woman in her late forties began to feel extreme anxiety over what she thought was a simple problem. A friend had asked her for money. In response, she went to the bank and made out a money order, but she became so anxious that she could not mail it. The problem persisted for weeks; each time she attempted to mail the money order, there was a flare-up of tension. As she explored the problem in therapy, she stated, 'I should give the money' (Parent ego state), and 'I want to give the money' (Adult ego state), 'but I am too nervous' (Child ego state). When at last she got in touch with her anxiety, she unleashed a torrent of angry feelings against the friend.

Before the therapeutic work, she knew what the Parent and Adult ego states said; but in the sessions she uncovered her hostility, and as she did so her anxiety subsided. I was fascinated to see this woman, who had a rigid character style, come to terms with her anxiety as quickly as she did. However, immediately after the exposé of her anger, she clicked it off. Reverting to her former state of indecision, she said to me, 'Now, Doctor, what shall I do? Shall I give my friend the money, or not?' It was pathetic to observe that this patient almost instantaneously buried the anger she had been looking at a few moments before and reverted to her indecision. Apparently her anger was so unacceptable, and the uncovering of it even for a moment was so threatening, that it required instantaneous burial.

Crazy clean

The perfectionistic housewife may become 'crazy clean', keeping her house spotless and immaculate. She may even recognize the excessive nature of her dirt-searching. However, if she stops cleaning, she becomes nervous and anxious. Her excessive cleanliness is a way of controlling other people in the household and is really a mask of hostility. One person I know kept emptying ash-trays as she sat with company. Can you imagine how uncomfortable her guests felt as they smoked? The crazy-clean person does not recognize how angry and controlling her behaviour can be; she does not recognize that her need to be crazy clean is an attempt to control her own hostility by controlling others. When she stops her frantic cleaning, her anxiety begins to erupt, revealing under the tension a load of rage. Work addicts are similar in many ways to the crazy-clean housewife, feeling comfortable only when they are busy, busy, busy and physically active. Physical activities have the double function of working off tensions and controlling the scream within.

Habits or rituals

I would first like to clarify what I mean by rituals. To me, they are the repetition of silly and petty actions that you recognize as inappropriate but which you seem compelled to perform. If you try to stop them, you become nervous and tense. Frequently these rituals involve organizing things in a special way: putting your clothes in just the right position beside your bed, getting tense if your shoes are not just right, or checking and rechecking the doors, the windows and the furnace.

Jean was a young married woman plagued by night rituals. Before bedtime she had to check the stove, the doors and the windows – not once or twice, but many times. She recognized how ridiculous it was, but if she stopped she became too tense to sleep. This repeated checking took place every night. Jean's personality was overly nice and excessively moral, and she was never angry. She was a compulsive person and suffered from severe and recurrent sieges of anxiety and depression.

As she progressed in therapy, she became aware of an intensely angry and jealous Child within her that hated her younger sister and even had fantasies of killing her. She recognized the intense jealousy over her mother's affection for her younger sister. Eventually she was able to feel, ventilate and accept her hostility, but it was not easy. As she became aware of her jealous, angry Child, she was able to accept it, and to direct it in ways better suited to her life. As she continued to use her anger, her rituals decreased to tolerable levels.

Obsessions

Have you ever become involved with repetitive thoughts that whirl around in your head like a broken record? I am sure we all have had some such experience of what is called obsessional thinking. You might find yourself brooding and worrying, recognizing that it is excessive and disproportionate, yet unable to stop. In depression, the obsessions involve continual brooding and ruminating about the 'I', and always in a self-belittling way. It is as if your contact with the external world had been broken, leaving you totally involved with your own unpleasant and detestable self.

Your obsessional thoughts might be about any topic: financial problems, marriage difficulties, death or accidents. Some people keep worrying that their children are going to become sick and die. They even have repetitive thoughts about hurting their children. While these thoughts are really alien to the way they live, the anxiety accompanying the thoughts becomes quite disabling. A female patient told me that every time her husband was late in getting home from the office she was obsessed with the idea that he had been killed in an accident.

Ruminative, obsessional thinking is another technique for controlling anger. The person uses records of irrelevant thoughts to control resentments he feels towards his environment. The more intense the brooding and the worrying, the larger the mass of angry feelings that needs to be submerged. Some obsessions I have seen in females take the form of fits of jealousy in which they accuse their husbands of infidelity although they know it is not true. The interesting thing about this behaviour is that the unwarranted jealousy allows the ventilation of anger over what is really an imagined situation. It appears that the real anger cannot be dealt with directly and needs some fictitious but concrete justification, such as manufactured ideas of infidelity.

Obsessed with sex

'Y' is obsessed with sex. She is a rigid, inhibited, compulsive woman who feels she has excessive sexual drives that must be satisfied lest she run wild sexually, attacking men. She recognizes that these ideas are totally out of character and yet she is preoccupied with them. Much of her life is planned around her sexual obsessions. Her husband must bring her to climax at regular intervals for her to function in her daily life. Sometimes he must spend hours, almost to the point of exhaustion, to give her satisfaction. She thinks certain foods are aphrodisiacs and avoids them, thus limiting her diet severely and losing much-needed weight.

'B' is obsessed with the thought that sex is dirty. Anything remotely connected with it, any thought or act, produces extreme anxiety and cleaning rituals. Even after a sex dream, she will wash the linen and night clothes and spray her room. She needs constant reassurance that sex is clean, but her old ideas always return to haunt her. She recognizes their inappropriateness, yet is compelled by her anxiety to perform her cleaning rituals. The concern over sex goes on and on, and frequently it is a whole day's preoccupation.

It is ironic that obsessions with sex are really masks of anger, and that the basis of the anger is totally unrelated to sex.

Miss Goody Two Shoes: pseudomutuality

Some perfectionistic people come across as overly friendly, excessively nice, and 'just too sweet'. Their interest in you is rather insincere and seems overdone. If you have ever encountered someone like this in a social situation, you will recall your discomfort and your irritation with the obvious insincerity. In a sense, the phony smile is a denial of the person's hostility. It is as if he were wearing a sweat shirt that says, 'See how nice I really am.' Unconsciously, he has buried his anger by reaction formation, by becoming the opposite of what he really is. His extreme niceness is false friendliness – pseudomutuality.

Sometimes when you meet a person like this whom you have not seen for a long time, he may greet you heartily. His back-slapping will seem a little out of place, and he may end up with, 'We should get together soon.' Next time this happens, try taking out your date book and asking, 'When ?' (This suggestion may come from my mischievous Child!)

The overly nice person basically comes across in one of two roles: either as the benevolent, solicitous and over-protective Parent, or as the obsequious, compliant, obedient and apologetic Child. The excessively loving Parent, while he appears sweet on the surface, is, by the very way he speaks down to you, really reflecting hostility. His insinuation that you need such a great big protective mother in order for you to function defines your relationship with him as that of an inferior. Under the ever-loving, ever-present, big-breasted Mother might be an angry bitch of a Kid.

Then there is the fellow who comes across as a nice, nice Child, trying to be liked by all. As an adaptive Child, he attempts to be what other people expect him to be. If you are talking to him, he may come out with excessive 'Yes, sirs', usually in a soft, quiet-spoken way. He seems to believe that the humble will inherit the earth, but he does not know that the aggressive types rule it. He may be the 'milk-toast' who backs off from arguments, is always agreeable and does not assert himself.

It is not so much what these super-nice people say that gets us; it is the tone of voice, the excessive softness, the over-solicitous manner, the big friendly smile, the total lack of sincerity. The person with the pseudomutuality personality, whether he comes across as the benevolent Parent or as the obedient Child, has one underlying dynamic: he is using his niceness to suppress and control the anger within him.

Deadness

One of the most terrible tragedies about the curse of perfectionism is the resulting emotional deadness. Many compulsive people have suffocated their feelings; as they speak, their words are blunted and without emotion. They may be aware that they are not getting much of a kick out of life. Their capacity for pleasure is greatly impaired. However, although they are aware that they do not feel very intensely, they are usually troubled by deep pain within, by restlessness and tension alternating with recurring periods of depression. They may seem to be cold, aloof and without warmth, and to be suppressing their alive Child. Often when they see the playful, rebellious Child in others they condemn it. They probably will not admit it, but their sex drive is down; the desire is much less than normal, and the pleasure from orgasm is reduced. They have lost their ability to be angry, dislike outbursts of temper and frequently say things like 'You should control yourself.' Despite their denial of anger, they may occasionally have rage explosions in which anger bursts forth, but this only strengthens their belief that anger is dangerous. They repress it further and submerge it, but it explodes again at a later date, usually precipitated by some minor incident. One 'dead' patient summed up his feelings quite well when he said, 'I would just like to say "no". I either swallow my anger or explode and feel like belting someone.'

Summary of the curse of perfectionism

The perfectionist is a 'tight ass', rigid and inflexible. Frequently when he thinks that he is in his logical Adult role, he is really a big, demanding, critical Parent. His Parent has sneaked in to rule his personality and to dominate yours. He sets extremely high standards of performance for himself and expects you to live up to his unrealistic expectations. He is the most subtle Now I've Got You, You Son of a Bitch player that I know.

Unfortunately, the perfectionist is his own worst enemy. His critical Parent is attacking viciously and demands that his Child live up to his unrealistic demands. As a result, the Child ego state has been submerged; its feelings are squeezed and suppressed, so that he often appears cold, aloof and unemotional. The ultimate curse of perfectionism is the severe kick that the Parent inflicts upon its own Child. Tragically we see the perfectionist, time and time again, suffer crippling anxiety and periods of disabling depression.

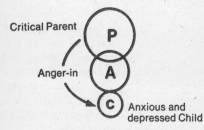

The curse of perfectionism

4 The inner self

10 'Me too'

Me Too in me

As patients with the faces and masks of anger enter into the arena of group psychotherapy, they begin a journey into the unconscious mind. The vehicle by which they take this strange and difficult trip is Here and Now psychotherapy, primarily Transactional Analysis and Gestalt Therapy. Often the progress is slow and tedious and they seem to be taking one step forward and two back. Occasionally there are brilliant and dramatic breakthroughs into self-awareness, followed by a complete disappearance of painful symptoms of emotional illness. However, the effects of sudden success may quickly disappear, and the symptoms will return another day and have to be worked through again and again and again.

Gradually the layers of anger are peeled away and the hostilities are exposed and experienced. They may break through explosively or seep through with barely any intellectual awareness of the frustrations. The resentments and angers are emotions of the present. They are occurring in the day-to-day life of the individual but have been dealt with ineffectively and neurotically. As we explore the angers, we find them connected with problems of daily living, with the frustration of our natural needs for food, safety, clothing, shelter, sex and territory. Often we discover, in the here and now, angers resulting from basic problems that have plagued us for years, that date from a much earlier age and yet still persist in a hidden or displaced way in the present. These most important problems stem from the ways we meet our needs, especially our need for love, affection, attention and recognition. They are not problems limited to emotional illnesses, but ones that all of us must cope with as we grow from infancy to adulthood. In adolescence, when we leave our families and enter the community, these core difficulties often reach a crisis as we strive to attain a level of independence and personal identity. They are commonly found, lying unresolved, in most forms of mental illness. In the perspective of

Transactional Analysis, they are centred within the Child ego state.

The Child within us today has many faces, showing the full range of feelings from pleasure and warmth to anger and pain. One aspect of this Child I call the clinging, helpless, dependent, demanding Child ego state. Having an intense need for affection, attention and recognition, it frequently yells in a hidden way, 'Give it to me,' 'I need,' 'Mommy,' or 'Me too.' The yell may be so disguised that we will not be aware of the emotional

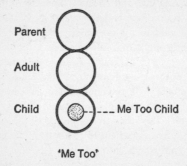

Parent

Adult

Child —— Me Too Child

'Me Too'

hunger within. When these needs are not met or are frustrated, the Child responds with sadness, anxiety and anger. Look at young children and see how they get angry when their needs are not met. Of course, they are conscious of their wants, and of their resentments to their frustrations. All of us, to some degree, have this kind of Child still present within us. Your dependency-demands may sneak in without your awareness. However, when your needs for stroking are not met, rage develops.

Some of us have greater needs than others, and some of us have difficulty in meeting any of our requirements. Some of us are still searching for a magical Mother to fill the needs that were never met when we were children. Eric Berne called this 'Waiting for Santa Claus'. I think it is an angry-dependent relationship that, when unmasked, is found at the base of most emotional difficulties. The greater the demands, the greater the frustration and the greater the anger towards those who fail to meet the needs.

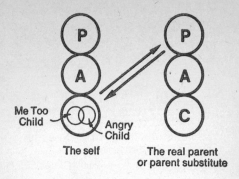

Me Too Child

Angry Child

The self

The real parent
or parent substitute

Hostile-dependent relation

The tighter the two hands are clenched together in an intense dependency bond, the greater the rage and hostility. The anger can be used to cut the bonds of the intense relationship, and, as it cuts through the dependency-needs, the anger becomes self-abolishing and disappears. As soon as you let go of Mother's hand, the anger you feel towards her tends to disappear. But there is a risk: now you need to become independent and self-sufficient. Can you grow up?

In an angry-dependent relationship in which a person has difficulty handling his excess of hostility, perhaps you can imagine the intensity of the emotional illness that follows. It is a difficult problem with many complicated aspects. I think that at some point in our lives we start to give up making such demands upon others and begin to take some personal responsibility for our needs; in other words, we 'go and get it ourselves', or 'get on with living'.

As we grow older, how do we give up making demands on others and begin to look after ourselves? Our parents may have felt that, by frustrating our needs as children, they would teach us to be responsible for ourselves. However, I believe that as a child grows up, if his parents help him to feel more and more OK about himself, he will take on more responsibility with pleasure and excitement, and will not have to be forced to be independent. If our parents have failed to do this, then we have the job of doing it ourselves. We may bring in the Adult to recognize our abilities, strengths and needs. We may bring in our nurturing Parent to love and support us and make us feel OK.

If we are not really demanding of others, then certainly we produce less hostility. This angry-dependent relationship, which I feel is hidden, is usually the chief cause of an excessive production of hostility. Coming to terms with the angry-dependent relationship means as a rule that a person moves from one level of dependency-craving to another – to the stage that I call an independent heterosexual relationship and functioning. On one level of angry-dependence, the person is constantly responding to others as a dependent child would respond to an omnipotent parent. When he advances to the higher level of adult heterosexual functioning, he assumes responsibility and learns to deal with his various growth needs. Now he has a sense of independence, a clearer identity and the enjoyment of accomplishment. At this point he has to deal more realistically with life and with the problems of sexuality, occupation and interdependence.

Growing fat

The causes of obesity are multiple, but I am convinced that in some people overeating reflects the degree to which their psychological hunger for affection has not been satisfied. One woman plagued by obesity was able to lose weight with relative ease as she worked through her hostile-dependent conflicts in therapy. For the first time in her life she was aware of her Me Too Child and was able to go and ask for some 'tender loving care' from friends and relatives. Despite her real-life stresses of a financial loss and a threat of separation from her husband, she was able to grow psychologically; she was getting some needs met, learning to cope with some dependency frustrations and losing weight at the same time. She recognized that her desire for food paralleled her state of loneliness, and that food was a substitute for affection.

In depression, you may swing drastically from complete loss of appetite to over-eating. Many people in a lonely, emotionally starved claiming depression eat voraciously. In many self-blaming depressions, when the anger is excessive and turned inwards, people are eating themselves up emotionally, with a marked loss of appetite and a rapid loss in weight.

Me Too in communication
Dumping
The cry of the hungry Child can often be heard in a 'dumping syndrome'. You may have a friend who continually calls you to dump his problems on you. It is a purely self-involved kind of talking, a conversation in which he tells you his difficulties without having any regard for you. His hidden hope is that you will respond as a 'magical, rescuing Parent'. In group therapy, dumping is often done and other patients recognize the totally helpless, dependent plea of the one who dumps.

Me Too and you
Many times, the Me Too – this clinging, demanding, self-centred aspect of ourselves – creeps into a person's conversation in a manner that is obvious to others, yet is beyond his awareness. I am sure you have had the experience, when hearing someone talk about an incident, of immediately recalling a similar situation in your own life. Some people use such social interchange solely to deal with their own lives, ignoring other people. For example, a man tells you something about his children; you recall a similar incident about your children, which you relate back. If he tells you about a particular doctor he saw, you talk about your illness or operation. If he talks about any sort of difficulty, you respond with something personal. In a sense, what you are doing in response to the other person's communication is repeating, 'Me too, me too!' Of course, if you have had this experience with someone, you can realize the intense self-involvement of the Me Too reaction. This form of communication excludes the other person and is concerned only with the self.

However, the Me Too in conversation can also be an expression of normal intimacy and sharing. To establish closeness with someone, you have to share your personal life with him. In other words, the Me Too that is narcissistic and self-involved is using a topic of discussion for the sole purpose of talking about the 'I'. The Me Too that leads to intimacy uses the 'I' and the topic to talk to the other person and include him in the dialogue. If we combine the I-thou, the content of conversation, and the here and now, we produce a blend of empathy and intimacy in an exciting, rewarding form of social interaction.

Me Too and intimacy

True intimacy involves your Me Too Child with the other person's Me Too Child in a process of give and take. A young married woman who was in an acute panic in the middle of the night ran to her mother's home. It looked on the surface as if her helpless Child were running to her mother's Parent for mothering and nurturing; yet she and her mother were able to relate on the Child-to-Child level, each giving part of herself in an intimate way. Mother listened warmly, reflected some of her own anxieties, and shared with her daughter some of her personal problems. She did not give advice. By giving part of herself, the mother helped her daughter to find her own solutions. There was relief of anxiety, and both mother and daughter enjoyed the intimacy.

Me Too in marriage

Some women relate to men basically as dependent Child to powerful Parent and are unable to form a good sexual relationship. Such relationships can be frictionless, as long as each decides to maintain the Child-to-Parent relationship. However, should one change, conflicts may develop in the marriage.

A young woman who was married to a very compulsive, confident man tended to relate to him from her helpless Me Too Child. However, in this position many of her demands were frustrated, and she began to feel hostility. She turned this anger in upon herself, producing a depression and precipitating a need for psychiatric treatment. Through therapy she became aware of her intensely demanding, hungry Child. This awareness gave her the ability to decide to switch to the Adult role. Of course, this produced conflicts within the marriage, because now there was a crossed-communication pattern. She wanted to react to her husband on an equal level, but he kept regarding her as a little girl. At last report, she was very sad and was seriously considering whether her marriage could survive. She was healthier, but the marriage now seemed unsuited to her needs. Both she and her husband faced the difficult job of adjusting to her personality change.

Another woman, married to a professional man, kept appealing to him from her helpless Child, seeking him as an all-powerful Parent. But every time he came in to rescue her she criticized him for treating her as a child. Her helpless plea in the marriage, of course, was really an angry manoeuvre, and her main intention in using it was to attack her husband. When she became aware of the dynamics of their marriage fights, she also recognized that she could switch to an Adult-to-Adult level with her husband. She could solve the angry-Child-to-Parent relationship that still existed in her life and that she had transferred to her husband. She could even let her angry Child out more directly, rather than having to play the devious, manipulative game of 'Rescue Helpless Me'.

A healthy marital relationship is not rigid. It flows in an open, direct way from ego state to ego state. Sometimes it can be Adult to Adult. At other times, one person will nurture the Me Too Child of the other person. And sometimes the Me Too Child of both will simply play, have sex, and relate with closeness.

Lonely in a crowd

Our Me Too needs for recognition and attention are like physical hunger. A good meal of stroking is fine, but the urge for affection returns within a short time in a new situation. Even with old friends, constant recognition of each other is necessary for the satisfying of stroking needs. I recently returned from a convention, where my anxiety in a crowd of strangers had risen and my sense of aloneness had seemed to be aggravated by the friendliness of the gathering. The Child within me resented the lack of affection and attention. I was 'lonely in a crowd'. Making some meaningful contacts with new people and reaffirming a few old acquaintances gradually filled my stroking needs, and I began to relax with a sense of pleasure and exhilaration. I then recognized that others craved stroking as well, but masked their needs under a guise of flirtation and sexuality.

Me Too and God

Many people indirectly reveal their Me Too relationships by their religious attitudes and beliefs. A patient in the midst of a severe depressive illness kept having fantasy conversations with God, saying, 'Why do you let me suffer so?' Essentially she was blaming God for her distress. Another patient at the height of distress kept crying to God for help and relief from her emotional pain. These are two examples of the ultimate in the dependent Child game of Waiting for Santa Claus – waiting for deliverance by God.

11 Helpless and angry games

Helpless-and-angry-Child-to-Parent games

'Ain't It Awful?', 'Poor Me' and 'Why Don't You – Yes But' are dependent-Child-to-Parent games that occur in interplay between people – usually, as we saw earlier, without their awareness. People play these games to get attention. A woman I referred to earlier kept a diary of all her misfortunes and would frequently replay the record of Ain't It Awful, or Poor Me or Look What Happened to Me in My Life. She was really in her whining Child ego state, looking for sympathy.

I have seen the game of Ain't It Awful played in a group, with a somewhat different outcome. There was a young lady who kept crying the blues and, of course, she hooked some benevolent, rescuing Parent within the group. It was interesting, though, that when the Parent came in to help, the Child then rejected the Parent's suggestions. So although the plea was helplessness, the message really turned out to be an angry rejection of authority. This is one of the ways the Child's angry dependency persists in adult life in a masked way.

Why Don't You – Yes But is a fascinating game that can waste hours of communication, as well as hours of psychotherapy. For example, a woman in a group of people presents this problem: 'My husband doesn't make love to me any more.' Someone in the group responds with, 'Why don't you try a sexy perfume?' She replies, 'Yes, but I'm allergic to perfume.' Someone else says, 'Why don't you try "A"?' To which she responds, 'That is a great idea, but I can't use "A".' The game goes on indefinitely. Note that the woman seems to be pleading for advice from the people around her, but rejects every suggestion with a 'yes but'.

Observe the person who replies with 'yes but' and you may discover that he sometimes reveals his game by giving a slight smile or laugh following the frustration he has helped to create in the interchange. Underlying this game is a message that says, 'My Child will get all of you Parent bastards,' or words to that effect. The idea of giving up all of these Child-Parent interactions can be very threatening. First, the person has to become aware of them. Then, having done so, he has to make a decision to change. Once he does this, he is faced with new needs, new difficulties – and, hopefully, the reward of new pleasures.

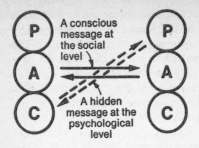

Helpless-and-angry-Child-to-Parent games

The 'Blaming Game', or 'If It Weren't for You', is basically the helpless Child blaming the Parent in others for emotional troubles. This is very common in marriages in which each spouse tends to blame the other for the conflicts. When this kind of couple comes to a psychiatrist, they usually play 'Court-room', asking the doctor to judge the guilty party.

The power of silence

Silence is a powerful form of communication. A cloak of many expressions, it may be a silent scream for help, but frequently is an angry Child-to-Parent game. Some people remain basic-ally silent in social situations. They speak very little, perhaps only when spoken to, and rarely give anything of themselves spontaneously. Their verbal response to an approach is usually evasive and abrupt, sometimes even defensive. Such people are consciously afraid of the risks of speaking. They feel a danger of self-exposure, for they have such a low opinion of themselves that to speak up would be like 'putting their penis on the block'. Some think they may reveal unacceptable feelings that would be rejected by others. Silence seems to be a safe way of participating.

However, as we strip the layers away and get down to the

awareness of the real self with such silent people, we often find hostility. Silence is another passive and evasive, but masked, expression of resentment. One young woman recognized her extreme anger towards me, the psychiatrist, as she got in touch with her silent self. She had been determined never to speak in the group and in that way to 'screw the psychiatrist up'. She had also thought of sitting in the group and reading a book while other people talked. There was a man in the same group who would withdraw and (as he later told me, privately) deliberately focus his thoughts on mental mathematics – a quiet way of saying to the rest of us, 'Go to hell!' Again, undneath a cloak of silence there was an angry Child rebelling in a passive way against the authority represented by the group, or by me, the psychiatrist. In a sense, the man was really trying to deal with his teen-age rebellion. He handled it in such a stubborn, passive, evasive way, however, that he never grew.

The Rope Trick

In one of my groups, a professional woman in the field of social sciences described her extremely unhappy relationship with her ageing mother. She complained that her mother continually made demands on her and would not allow her to grow up and live as an independent woman. As we re-enacted this scene in psychotherapy, I played the role of the mother, holding on to one end of a piece of rope while the woman held on to the other. I then asked her to re-enact what she felt was her relationship with her mother. With intense emotion, she yelled at me to let go. She pulled with all her strength on her end of the rope, but I did not let go. I was amazed at the violence and intensity of the struggle and at the outpouring of emotions as she screamed and yelled to me to let go. It was a number of minutes before she suddenly realized that she could let go of her end of the rope. This was an intensely symbolic move for her, for it was she herself who was in a position to let go, in this angry-dependent relationship with an ageing mother. Some time later her relationship with her mother changed. She recognized that she was in a more OK position, that her self-worth had gone up. She felt more like a total human being because she had given up the angry-dependent relationship and had switched to the Adult heterosexual level.

On seeing the Rope Trick demonstrated by another patient in the group, a young man burst into tears. He felt that his parents, a long time ago, had let go of their end of a loving relationship with him. When he was a baby, the family had been deserted by his father, and he felt that his mother had never really loved him. He cried uncontrollably as he felt his huge, hungry Child that had been starving from a very early age. With this awareness of himself, he could now feel needs that had never been met and that still persisted in an intense and demanding way. This deep sense of loneliness had been present for a long time, and he had been in a 'claiming depression' off and on for many years. Now that he had real awareness of his hungry Kid, he could take it to places where it might be fed.

Work and school failure

It is surprising to find in many work and school failures that it is not the patient's intelligence or ability to use logic that is faulty. I often find in such cases a form of unconscious conflict between the Parent and Child ego states. It is as if the Parent within you says, 'You should work,' or 'You should do your school work,' and the Me Too Child inside you says 'No!', rebels and fails. Stating it more simply, I have found that if people can change their attitude to work from an 'I should' to an 'I want' they can often succeed in coming to terms with a neurotic conflict. Sometimes it is necessary not only to resolve the internal Child-Parent struggle but also to deal with a real-life child-parent struggle. As you emancipate yourself from the fight within you and with those around you, you can make progress in school or in work and let your Adult guide you along paths your Child feels like following.

Two of the most flagrant examples of work failure I have seen, strangely enough, have been in university teachers in the field of psychiatry. One man, with whom I was working in a group, was telling me about his general activities, and in my Adult voice I asked, 'Are you still working?' At that moment, his face, which had carried a look of depression, broke into a

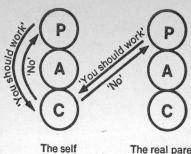

The self   The real parent
or parent substitute

smile; as he identified the smile, he was aware of his mischievous, defiant Child who was really yelling at me. He recognized that he thought my Adult question about his work was really a Parent injunction that he should work, and his smiling Child was saying 'I won't,' opposing any Parent message that I might send him. He also became aware of his angry Child defying the internalized demand of his Parent, which said, 'You should work.' This man is still trying to resolve his problem. But the second teacher overcame his work failure, which was a serious problem preventing him from getting tenure at his university, simply by switching his personal work attitude from a 'should' to a 'want'.

A brilliant man in his late forties considered himself a failure. Despite his high IQ, he had failed to complete his formal education and he had not found any meaningful work. He went from job to job, unhappy, and was frequently unemployed. He was usually in financial difficulty and was anxious and depressed about his social predicament. We found in therapy that his angry Child ego state frequently contaminated his Adult. His Adult wanted to work, but his Child saw work as a Parental demand made by society, and it rebelled. The only cure for such a man would be to isolate his angry Child, and prevent it from interfering with his Adult. Then he might be able to create a rewarding way of life for himself.

Anxiety, with its agitation and unrealistic fears, is a frequent cause of work failure, since it adversely affects the ability to

Angry Child
contaminates
the Adult

Angry Child
is separated from
the Adult

Problem   Cure

perform. Another common emotional cause of under-achievement at school or work is depressive illness. A patient finds it increasingly difficult to think, concentrate and function, because he is struggling under a burden of mental sluggishness and apathy caused by depression. The loss of motivation may be misinterpreted as a school or work problem, while the underlying depression remains hidden.

Risk of independence

Many people keep an intensely dependent relationship going, not so much because of its joys or rewards as through fear of the dangers of assuming independence. After all, growth involves new problems connected with sexual identity, sexual involvement, interdependence with others and taking responsibility for yourself. Occasionally, I see people maintaining this kind of helpless, clinging dependency because they will not face the rage they feel in the relationship. But once the anger is faced, they can free themselves and start to grow into a position of independence. Sometimes I wonder why people want to be independent. The answer is, of course, that there is a fine sense of fulfilment in producing for yourself; the value of the 'I' goes up, and there are many good feelings of satisfaction and pleasure.

Sex – a growth risk

A young girl who had been mentally ill for some years had an intense feeling of dependency on everyone in her environment. As she became aware of her problem and began to deal with it, she became panic-stricken over her sexual identity. She recalled that in her early childhood her mother had condemned all signs of sexuality. As an adult woman, this patient had no real concept of any sexual identity. She really did not know whether she felt like a man or a woman. Staying on a Child-Parent level in her environment had helped her to avoid this extremely threatening question. Giving up her dependency needs and emancipating herself to move to the heterosexual level produced intense anxiety and fear, for now she had to deal with the opposite sex and clarify her role as a woman.

12 Growing up

Accepting your helpless Child

Getting in touch with the attention-seeking Child within you – feeling it, experiencing it and accepting it – allows you to grow. There is a concept of polarity in which, by accepting one aspect of yourself, you allow the emergence of its opposite. Reowning your dependence paradoxically opens up your sense of independence. This swing from dependence to independence allows for the emergence of the healthy state of interdependence with people.

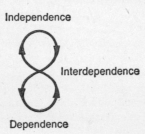

The Boiler Theory that I talked about earlier holds true in dealing with your helpless Child. A certain unmarried social worker attempted to hide her own needs and always responded like a rescuing Parent to the hurts of her clients. However, whenever a man showed her affection, her lonely Child burst through, usually in an incongruous way, producing some self-destructive behaviour such as inviting someone to seduce her when she did not really want sex at all. Seeing her needs explode in such an unsatisfactory way increased her conviction that they were not acceptable, and she tried to hide them even more completely. This increased the anxiety and frustration, but did not prevent the hungry Child's explosions. Of course, the answer was for her to accept her needs more openly, from moment to moment, and from situation to situation, in order to avoid the volcanic eruptions of her emotional hunger.

Some people deny that they have any dependency needs, and only come across in the Parent role: totally independent and with a big sign on the chest reading, 'I need no one.' These people form unsatisfactory relationships, being able to respond to you only as a Parent to your needy Child. Rarely can they share any of their intimate hurts and frustrations with you, in the kind of trusting communication that is necessary for a close and sincere relationship.

The compulsive person with the curse of perfectionism has a big, magic-seeking Me Too Child. It is almost totally beyond his awareness, and he normally appears in the opposite role – an authoritarian, independent role. When the big, critical Parent is stripped away, the hungry Child is exposed, becomes part of the real self and may be free to ask for stroking directly rather than through the mask of a claiming depression.

Teen-agers often overdo the independence role, trying to deny that they have any dependency strivings. Of course, some teen-agers put on a 'tough guy' look that is a reaction formation (an opposite reaction) to the way they feel. One teen-age girl, who was a lesbian 'Butch', had a tough masculine character, 'with balls'; this was a defence against her dependent Child ego state, which said, 'Please like me.' When she was a little girl, her Me Too part was never accepted by her parents. Today she is a tough, aggressive woman, using her homosexuality to deny her dependency. Of course, the drive for independence is exciting and growth-producing, but true independence can only be achieved by accepting your dependency as well.

An exciting example occurred with a young social worker who came across in groups as a critical authority and an independent professional. During an encounter in which her husband stroked her face and talked to her as a loving parent to a child, she burst into tears. She cried as she became aware of her emotionally hungry, attention-seeking Child that she had always denied, and she allowed her husband to comfort her. From this time on, she began to acknowledge, not only that she was an authority looking after other people's needs, but also that she, too, had a hungry Child who wanted attention and had a right to expect it. Strangely enough, with her acceptance of her dependency needs, her femininity and sexuality increased. Sex became more fun for her, and thinking of herself as a sexual woman made her feel good. Much to her surprise, many people were able to read this new picture she had of herself, and men began to approach her flirtatiously; in her work, she was surprised to find men responding to her as a sexy woman.

For me, it is an exciting aspect of personality growth that by facing and accepting disowned parts of yourself, such as your dependency and your anger, you also open up areas like sexiness. This is an extra reward for widening the scope of your personality, bringing you even closer to the fulfilment of your total personality potential.

Stroke for growth
The first act
A single woman, troubled with obesity for most of her life, had slimmed down in the course of a year of group psychotherapy. About a year later she returned to the group, depressed. She had fallen in love with a married man, who, even though he admitted his love for her, had decided to stay with his wife and end their relationship. The woman responded with intense sadness, which she recognized as quite realistic; at the same time, however, she began to overeat and within two months had gained more than twenty pounds.

During one depressed morning in bed, she experienced her emotionally hungry Child. She recalled her childhood and visualized herself as a little girl of seven. Her father, disabled by a war injury, was paralysed and she had never seen him walk. He was a bitter man, so involved in his own suffering that he gave her no affection. Her mother was a martyr and devoted herself totally to the father's suffering. She saw herself as a lonely child, whose major excitement consisted of running to the corner store, buying cake, and gorging herself. She had become a fat little girl, through the only source of 'feeding' available in this troubled family.

Her awareness of the past was the 'first act', the first feeling of emotional hunger and its ways of satisfaction. She recognized that these patterns persisted and had flared up again at the loss of the romance. With this experiential awareness of her neurotic pattern of obesity, she worked through the upset.

A crisis, with its pain and suffering, can be a potential for regression and mental illness. Paradoxically, it may alternatively serve as an opportunity to work through an old neurosis and to grow in emotional stature.

The best way to deal with your attention-seeking Child is, first, to recognize it and experience it. Then you will have the free choice of where, when and how to use it. You may recognize places where the needs cannot be met and where the demands are excessive. You may also realize that, by giving to other people, you are also vicariously gratifying your own needs. The second important step is to allow your benevolent Parent to love the Child that is in you, to give affection internally and say such things as 'I like you.' Show your Child as much love and affection as you might show a small child in your home. Thirdly, and most important, do not play the game of Kick Me when you realize that you have a hungry Child within you. Remember that healthy emotional growth requires positive stroking.

Accepting your own dependency needs will allow for freedom of flow between dependence, interdependence and independence – a flexibility of personality that responds to changing events of living. For example, you need your dependent part to relate with intimacy and warmth to the dependent part of others. By accepting all your roles on the dependency-independency scale, you may become a sincere, loving human being.

Transference resolution

In therapy, many people solve the problem of their dependency demands simply by coming to terms with the relationship between themselves and the psychiatrist. This is called the resolution of transference. The patient begins to build up patterns of behaviour towards the psychiatrist similar to those he felt and still feels towards his parents. Regardless of any of the patient's complaints upon coming to therapy, resolving this transference can in itself help him to grow into a healthier personality. It is very important for both patient and psychiatrist to be as open and honest as possible about the way they feel towards each other, because this might be the crux of treatment.

Of course, the psychiatrist may accuse the patient of Waiting for Santa Claus as a defence against his own therapeutic failure and technical deficiency. A patient who is frustrated by his psychiatrist's limitations should confront him directly. A ventilation of anger in their relationship may solve the therapy conflict. (If it does not, the patient can search for another psychiatrist.) As an additional pay-off, voicing his irritation may help the patient to grow emotionally.

One instance of transference resolution involved two men who were dissatisfied with their progress in ridding themselves of their homosexual roles. They approached me in group therapy one day and said that they wanted to deal with the situation as intensively as possible. I asked them to express, even in an exaggerated way, how they felt as they sat with me in therapy. They both began to admit that they wanted me to change them, to 'wipe the slate clean' of their homosexuality. When I exaggerated my response and said, 'Hey, fellows, I just can't change you,' they began to laugh with pleasure – a laugh that we in the group recognized as completely inappropriate. Since I was apparently admitting my failure, they both laughed with pleasure. They then recognized that defeating me as a therapist was more important to them than solving their own problems. They were dealing with transference and with the Child-to-Parent relationship that they had not solved in their own lives and that was symbolically present, in the group setting, between them and me.

Their homosexuality, a symptom of their emotional illness, possibly could be treated if they could resolve their transference response to me. They really were angry defiant kids trying to 'get' father or mother. One man remarked that even in his homosexual fantasies he was passive and childlike, accepting what the other person, as the aggressor, did. He recognized that he was having increasing heterosexual feelings as he altered his relationship to me. He was feeling less like a helpless child relating to me as an authoritarian parent, and was relating to me on a more equal level. This was indicated by his behaviour in the group, where he was now able to speak in a spontaneous and assertive way with less concern about whether I agreed or disagreed with what he said.

It is a paradox. A patient comes to a psychiatrist asking to be cured; yet only when he learns to help himself will he recover. Of course, the psychiatrist guides the process of self-awareness, but the patient must decide himself that he wants to grow into a unique, responsible human being. It is like the story *The Wizard of Oz:* Dorothy, the Strawman, the Tinman and the Lion finally find the magical wizard, only to discover that they have within themselves what they had been seeking from him – the wisdom, the emotions and the courage they want.

Angry youth
I would like to deal here with one aspect of anger in youth – natural anger. From puberty into adolescence there is a normal flooding of sexual and aggressive feelings. Anger flows freely, and each person handles it according to his character style. Some young people have a conscience that restricts and represses their feelings, thereby producing anxiety, depression and alienation from friends and society, and possibly a turning towards drugs for relief and pleasure.

This is one reason why many young people are susceptible to emotional illness. The adolescent who does succumb seems to have a severely critical Parent ego state, perhaps even more critical than the real-life parents from whom it derived. The Parent ego state of the young person probably emerged with some critical messages such as 'Don't be sexy,' 'Don't masturbate,' or 'Don't be angry.' But the natural impulses may be so strong that the person feels that more controls are required, and his Parent responds by becoming more critical and repressive. In a sense, a strong Kick Me produces an internalization and suffocation of natural feelings, with a resulting syndrome of anxiety, despair and alienation. On the other hand, if feelings are expressed outwardly, there is a risk that sex will run rampant and that aggressive drives with the full range of hostility will be ventilated explosively. However, the maturing Adult ego state can usually handle these feelings in a socially acceptable way – sometimes through trial and error.

Emancipation

The teen-ager must fight to separate. He needs to rebel against his parents and the other authorities in his life in order to emancipate himself and form his own identity. The tighter the reins, the tougher the fight. The intensity of the message of revolt varies from generation to generation and is certainly high today. Although we condemn some of its more extreme manifestations, we must acknowledge that the emancipation of teen-agers is growth-expanding and exciting.

The rebellion of the young brings with it new ways of living that lead to higher and more humanistic relationships, with new and exciting possibilities for change. The young today have increased our humanism by stressing feelings of warmth, trust and intimacy and by playing down the supremacy of cold logic.

The destructive elements of the rebellion, such as the abuse of drugs and an increased crime rate, are, I hope, a small aspect of the movement and will tend to disappear. The older generation, in order to maintain its position, seems to look only at the extremely destructive parts of the rebellion and, I fear, throw out the baby with the dirty water. A teen-ager who can rebel in his own way rarely ends up mentally ill. However, repression and inhibition of the inner drive for independence often lead to anxiety and severe depression.

Most of the depressions in teen-agers revolve around the problems of separating from their parents. There is not only the fight to separate, but also the sadness of giving up old child-parent relationships. (Parents as well must face their own sadness and anger in the separation process.) Sometimes children have to separate physically from their parents in order to grow. Sometimes it is only later in life that they can come back to form a new relationship with their parents on a different level; sometimes they never return.

It is not uncommon for a parent, with marked concern, to call me about his depressed or withdrawn teen-ager, who seems to have given up participation in living, work or school. After the teen-ager begins to grow in the course of therapy, and to get in touch with his aggressive drive and his hostility, I often get a second call from the parent, who this time asks what has happened to his nice obedient child. He admits that the child may have been depressed, but says that he was at least obedient, kind and pleasant. Now, however, he seems to be a holy fighting terror. I agree that the teen-ager may not be easier to live with, but he is healthier and back on the road to normal emotional growth.

I think that the teen-ager's rebellion against the authority of his parents and the conventions and values of society is frequently an expression of his desire to break the bond of the hostile-dependent child-parent relationship, and that it is necessary if he is to emancipate himself fully and achieve a clear personal identity.

Don't grow up!

Some parents give their children script messages such as 'Don't grow up.' Of course, consciously, parents have only the highest goals for their children. But in a hidden way the Child of the parent relates to the Child of the child in a 'Don't leave me' manner. One widow, while encouraging her son to complete university and to go on in his profession, kept telling him that he was the only one she was able to talk to: a hidden message of 'Don't leave me' that she had been giving to him most of his life. Now that he was approaching manhood, he was plagued by feelings of anxiety related to an old hostile-dependent relationship with his mother. Even though the mother transmitted unhealthy messages to her son, it was up to him to decide whether to accept or reject the 'witch' messages.

Growing down

Some of the drug abuse I have seen is a cop-out. I see people facing life and its problems in basically two ways: using their aggressive drive with hostility to 'go to' a problem, or using it to withdraw and avoid the problem. I have observed that young people who abuse drugs are often doing so in order to 'go away' or escape. One young girl illustrated this vividly in a group meeting. She had been ill about eighteen months before with an intense depression and strong suicidal impulses, and had required hospitalization for a number of months. While I was sure that many of her problems were multi-causal, there was no doubt that the use of marijuana and LSD precipitated severe panic and depressive symptoms. For the last year, her depression had been less severe, with the help of prescribed tranquillizers and anti-depressants. Her participation in group psychotherapy was minimal: she was mostly silent and withdrawn. Then, one day, she spoke. She said she was quitting the group. She was bored with the therapy, bored with her family, bored with her friends and bored with her work. She was going to leave therapy, leave home, leave school and go to another city. When we explored the meaning of 'another city', we found that there really was nothing that she was 'going to'; it was more that she was 'going away'. In the midst of this she said she had made a decision to go back to drugs, because they made her feel happy and aware. I was really impressed (and so was she) with the fact that drugs were part of her total approach to existence – a withdrawal from living because of her boredom with life.

Boredom and apathy are frequently hidden forms of hostility, silent expressions of anger and resentment. Boredom results in avoidance and withdrawal; but, if this passive form of anger can be externalized, energy for creative activity can be released. Possibly there is nothing for this girl to 'go to' at the present time. To her, life seems without purpose or pleasure. She has no personal motivation for change, no great drive for achievement, no cultural or nationalistic goal. Maybe it is not easy to find something to 'go to', but her escape is a 'growing down' process. The predictable result is another bout of mental illness.

Talking down
Hostility to authority: power struggle
I am continually struck with the fact that, in most interactions, whenever one person assumes a purely authoritative Parent role the other person responds with anger or irritation. I find this especially true in my role as a psychotherapist. When I switch

into my authoritative role, even if I am the most benevolent of authorities, giving the best possible information, the patient usually responds with some form of hostility. He may fight back or he may withdraw, depending on the way he handles his anger. I think this is the most common conflict between parents and children, especially teen-agers, who resent parents' talking down to them. The next time you are talking and sense some discomfort in the relationship, especially with children or a teen-ager, check to see whether you are not in your Parent ego state. Listen to your 'shoulds', watch your index finger working and listen to the Parent voice inside your head. If you hear your Parent coming on strong, use a different form of relationship: switch to Adult, or try your Kid, or let your Adult and Kid speak together – it might be fun.

In Transactional terms, the authority problem occurs when one party, in his Parent ego state, relates to another as if he were a dependent child. However, the angry Child of the second person is usually hooked in response to this 'talking down'. Much of this kind of communication may be unconscious, with the authoritarian person believing that he is in his logical Adult role. The person who receives the power play also believes that

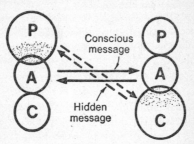

The authority relationship

he is in his Adult role, yet he may respond with anxiety or discomfort in the interaction, unaware that his angry Child has been hooked. (After all, what right has he to be angry with such a nice guy?)

I am certain that talking down produces many social, national and even international problems. In welfare or foreign aid programmes, when a government or agency gives help from its 'authoritative' position (and even though this help may be benevolent), it eventually generates some angry explosion of defiance from the recipient.

'Power parenting'

A 'smother mother' I know usually appears to be in her benevolent Parent role, taking over for everybody. She desperately tries to find solutions to their problems and to direct them towards happiness and mental health, yet her rescuing only hooks their resentments. They respond with anger to her authoritative ways. Her actions are really an angry gesture of her authoritative Parent, for she attempts to rob her children of their opportunity to become unique, independent individuals. The big-breasted Mother force-feeds her children *ad nauseam*.

Permissiveness

Many of us complain that permissive attitudes towards children are to blame for the troubles of youth. Permissiveness can be one of two different things. First, it can be withdrawal or disinterest – a lack of caring; parents sometimes get involved with themselves and, under a mask of permissiveness, ignore their children. Second, it can be caring and giving the child a chance to be a unique individual – true permissiveness, or intelligent neglect, whereby you refrain from coming on in the authoritative Parent role, talking down to the child and telling him what he should or should not do. True permissiveness is flexibility in using your Parent role to set limits when needed. It means relating at certain times on an Adult-to-Adult level and at other times on a Child-to-Child level, so that the youngster, through sharing with you, is able to assume responsibility for his own life.

The Karpman Triangle

One of the most exciting demonstrations of the process of the authority problem is found in the diagram reproduced here, called the Karpman Triangle. In most authoritarian relationships there is a power struggle, and usually the authoritarian person tries to be the rescuer of a victim who is helpless. If he fails, he becomes angry with the victim and so becomes his persecutor. As a persecutor, however, he is still in an authoritarian

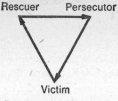

The Karpman Triangle

role, trying to change the victim. Yet even persecuting the victim fails, and suddenly the would-be-rescuer-turned-persecutor finds himself a victim of his own efforts.

It is extremely easy and quite tempting for a therapist to attempt to be a rescuer or persecutor of a patient who appears as a victim. Usually these authoritarian approaches fail, because, no matter how weak the victim may appear, he usually defeats the rescuer or persecutor. A good psychiatrist or social worker is essentially a facilitator, helping the patient to take charge of his own life. A good mental health councillor directs without attempting to control.

Falling off the pedestal

When you have a hostile-dependent relationship with people, you are essentially relating from your Me Too Child ego state to their authoritarian Parent. Sometimes in this role you are 'not OK', and you label others as 'experts' and 'super-OK'. You may feel inferior in their presence and cowed by the brighter, omnipotent cloak in which you have dressed them.

However, as you emancipate yourself from this form of relationship, your view of the God-like authorities changes. You recognize that, even though other people may know more than you, you can meet them on an equal level. You may recognize their ability and talent, yet also see some of their weaknesses and failings. Above all, as you mature, they seem to fall from the God-like pedestal on which you have placed them. You cease your hero-worship and see them as real people, as you grow in emotional stature. Then you have probably reached the position of 'I'm OK – you're OK'.

Many people in group therapy, in the relationship with me as their therapist, call me Dr Birnbaum. As they grow and emancipate themselves to a different level of communication with me, they often call me Jack. Our relationship changes and they can assert themselves independently and speak to me as a person who happens also to be a trained psychiatrist.

The process of emancipation

Here is a description of one way in which teen-agers achieve personal growth and identity.* The angry Child of the teen-ager attacks the parents, their values, ethics, cultural background and customs. It is really the Parent ego state of the parents that is being attacked. The parents over-respond to this attack, out of their own irrationality and prejudice, and the result is a battle that can last for days, weeks, months or even years. For example, when long hair first became popular, a father I knew slapped the face of his teen-age son because the boy would not have his hair cut. The angry Child of the teen-ager had become the provocateur of the parent, who then attacked as a persecutor. As the battle progressed in such cases, between provocateur (the child) and persecutor (the parent), at some point a new adult awareness enters into the picture. At this point the teen-ager may find his identity as an adult by emancipating himself from his parent. The parent may change as well, by modifying his standards and values. On a larger scale, this process of conflict between teen-ager and parent creates social and cultural change.

Depression of aloneness

An existential crisis occurs during the time of emancipation from your hostile-dependent relationships. When you are giving up your hidden demands upon your parents – demands that you frequently displace in other relationships – you begin to feel the

* Refer to the game called 'High and Proud' in Claude Steiner, *Games Alcoholics Play* (New York: Grove Press, 1971).

anxiety of separation and the depression of aloneness. Losing old ties leaves you temporarily alone and sad. However, it appears necessary to begin a quest for new relationships on a different level. The problem of 'Who am I ?' is in the foreground of a tension-filled crisis of identity. It is a time of inadequate emotional supplies from without, and of a need for reliance upon stroking from within. It is a period of stress that sometimes involves the risk of suicide. Tolerating the depression, staying with it and working it through allows for growth and self-reliance on a new level of Adult heterosexual functioning. The depression of aloneness is essentially a claiming depression, with or without awareness of the intense, painful emotional hunger.

Claiming depression
Our Me Too needs, like our physical hunger, require regular and meaningful feedings of sufficient quantity. Supply sources are available within our personality and in the external environment. We need both our own loving, benevolent, internal Parent ego state to positively stroke the Child from within and the external world of people to stroke us from without.

One of the first signs of stroke hunger is sadness; and, if intense and prolonged, it may become a claiming depression. Regardless of our stage of development or our chronological age, whenever we are deprived of basic emotional needs we respond with sadness and anger. If these are handled adaptively, we recognize our deprivation, and the anger may trigger us into action to fulfil our needs quickly and efficiently.

If the hungry cry and the 'cry anger' are beyond our awareness, we may react neurotically. We may suppress, ignore and deny our hunger. We may turn the anger in upon ourselves, in our frustration. The anger-in leads to a self-blaming aspect of our claiming depression. This neurotic circular depression may result in an intense self-perpetuating spiral that can be incapacitating – a full-blown emotional illness.

Summary

Our basic emotional-dependency demands – the part that says 'I want more, too much' – cannot be met completely and are bound to be frustrated. We react to this block with sadness and anger. The anger turned in results in a whole range of emotional illnesses (depression, anxiety, perfectionism etc), and we withdraw. The withdrawal only increases our needs, and we continue in a vicious circle of hostile-dependent relationships, often in a masked or hidden way. I think that the recognition and experiencing of our anger is the main mechanism by which we

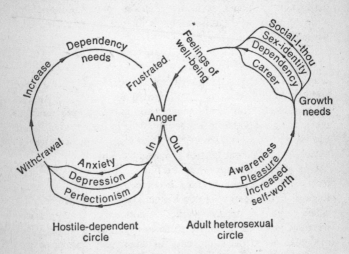

Hostile-dependent circle

Adult heterosexual circle

switch to the Adult heterosexual circle. With the awareness of our anger, we soon recognize our hidden wants. The awareness itself brings pleasure and self-confidence. Outwardly expressing our anger, rather than turning it in by way of a Kick Me, stops the blow to our self-esteem. We then begin to deal with growth requirements: the needs for independence and identity and sex, for work and career choice, for social living, and for love and affection (although these dependency needs are less than before). Hopefully, there are rewards of pleasure that keep us in this new circle of Adult heterosexual living. Of course, we will switch back and forth; but, the healthier we get, the more we remain on this upper level of mental health.

If I am OK with the Me Too part in me, then the chances are that I am going to be OK with you. If I am OK with the Me Too part in me, then I will be able to be close and warm with you. If you and I are both OK, then our relationship will stretch and grow with the expression and confrontation of our hostility here and now.

5 The expression of anger

13 Anger now!

Mind-Fucking

The above term, coined by Dr Fritz Perls, is not obscene; it is almost poetic. Dr Perls used the term to show how we put our ideas into other people's heads to explain their behaviour. He used the term in criticizing people and especially psychiatrists who inflict their own theories and interpretations upon suffering individuals. One depressed patient was told by a psychiatrist that he had a small-penis complex and that this was why he was depressed. The patient then walked around, with additional self-belittling fuel, feeling even more depressed and rejected. My purpose in using the term mind-fucking is to criticize the whole concept of the 'why' and 'because' of behaviour, and the over-emphasis we have placed on it.

People in group therapy especially tend to mind-fuck about other people's behaviour (Dr Berne called this the game of 'Play Psychiatry'). A depressed young woman confided to her group that she was keeping alive a fantasy of her baby, who had died several years before. She told us that she day-dreamed almost daily about the baby and had silent conversations with him. She described the intense love she felt for this child and the love the child showed her in return. After she had shared her fantasy with us, members of the group gave theories about why she was keeping this dead child alive. They all began mind-fucking. Some said that the baby was the only symbol of love in her life, since her other relationships were filled with hostility and hate. Some gave advice and suggested that she adopt another child. Even I began to intellectualize about the reasons, and the risks of giving up the fantasy. After we had mind-fucked the problem to death, I asked her to imagine the baby in the 'empty chair'.* As she played both parts, talking for herself and for the baby, she experienced a range of loving and sad feelings. Suddenly she became very angry and began to express strong resentment against the baby for dying and leaving her alone. When she had ventilated the reservoir of hidden anger, she

* See p 130, 'Bringing the Past into the Present'.

seemed relieved and was then able to say goodbye to the child. The fascinating thing for me and the group was that our intellectual attempts to analyse were so distant from the emotional solution the patient had found for herself.

Mental masturbation

Many of us, as we attempt to analyse our own behaviour, ask ourselves 'Why ?' as a form of self-criticism, such as 'Why did I do that stupid thing ?' It really is an internalized Kick Me. At other times we use the 'why' to intellectualize, to talk, as a smoke-screen for our own feelings. We use logic to avoid an emotion that we are experiencing at the moment. In other words we use our Adult and Parent ego states to suffocate the suffering Child within us. This self-analysis, or mental masturbation, often is brooding and upsetting, and it usually fails to bring relief from the symptoms. Sometimes we attempt to rationalize our behaviour and to examine the past in order to explain the present, and we may even try to predict the future. We are really avoiding the present situation – 'What am I doing right now ?'

'What am I doing right now?'

This is the question that introduced me to Here and Now therapy. I recall one most significant case that directed me to this concept of psychiatric treatment.

A psychologist consulted me for depression. He was a bright man in his early thirties and was well versed in Freudian psychiatry. In our first meeting I gathered the usual information about his past life. But I approached the second meeting with a new concept. I kept asking myself during the interview, 'What is going on between this man and me, here and now ?' He talked spontaneously, with considerable insight, about his distant and recent past, while I kept wondering what we were really doing with each other in the present. I occasionally interrupted him to ask how he felt at this very moment. While he seemed a little surprised at my interruption, he always responded, 'I am fine.' As he replied, I noticed that he looked comfortable and relaxed. Later in the meeting, he began to talk about his homosexual impulses and about his fear of being a homosexual. As he described his fears, I observed him again, very closely, and he appeared quite relaxed, semi-reclining in a big easy chair in my office. To confirm my observation, I again asked him, 'How are you feeling right now?' And again, somewhat surprised, he answered, 'Fine.' I then stated that I was puzzled by what seemed incongruous: he appeared relaxed while telling me about one of the most frightening concerns in his life – the fear of homosexuality. I said I had the impression that he was like a little boy, lying in the safety of my chair and feeling secure. He became angry and said that he was not there to depend on me like a helpless child. The meeting ended, and I booked another appointment for the next week. He left through the double doors dividing my consultation room from the waiting room, and left them both open. I called to him to return, pointed out that he had left two doors open, and told him that I wondered who he thought was going to close them. He looked around, saw that the secretary was not there, and then replied, 'I guess you will have to.' I then said, 'Are you sure you don't want me to take care of you?' He smiled and left, closing both doors.

On his next visit, I learned that his depression had lifted right after our previous session, and had not returned. In fact, he entered into group therapy to deal with his other problems and was depression-free for about a year. In one group session his depression returned. When another patient pointed out the emergence of his helpless Child, his depression lifted immediately.

It was experiences like this one in the Here and Now arena that led me to further exploration. This case demonstrated the Freudian idea of dealing with the transference (the relationship between patient and psychiatrist that resembled old patterns of behaviour). Traditional Freudian psychotherapy is prolonged, and I realized that communication patterns within the interview could be dealt with early in therapy and the duration of treatment shortened in this way.

I began to enlarge the Here and Now arena, by employing the Parent, Adult and Child ego states from Transactional Analysis, and self-awareness and the 'empty chair' from Gestalt Therapy. Like Dr Perls, I feel that you change by becoming more and more your authentic whole self. You change by facing your unpleasant conflicts and by reowning parts of your personality that you have projected upon others. When you have experienced and become aware of your total self, then you can use the Adult ego state as 'executive', with the job of integrating the parts within you. It directs and guides the expression of the Child, and checks the old recordings of the Parent to see whether they are relevant to today's living. The Adult blends the internal states with the external environment and helps give you flexibility and, let us hope, pleasure and satisfaction in your day-to-day existence.

Bringing the past into the present
Much of my therapy has involved the Gestalt technique of bringing the past into the present, usually through the device of the 'empty chair'. The 'empty chair' has enlarged the arena of Here and Now psychotherapy beyond imagination. The patient can imagine anyone – living or dead – to be sitting in an empty chair, and relate to him in an emotionally meaningful way. He could bring anyone from the past into the present. He could put an opposing part of his personality into the 'empty chair' and relate to himself and come to terms with his internal conflicts. He could even use a number of 'empty chairs' to represent different ego states (such as nurturing Parent, critical Parent, Adult, natural Child and adaptive Child) to explore his problem.

A simple example of how the Here and Now and the 'empty chair' can produce a rich emotional experience is the case of a young woman who was talking and telling the group how angry she was at her mother. When asked to imagine her mother in the 'empty chair' and talk to her, here and now, she responded with an intense cry for the mother's love she still wanted today. She was able to come to a decision that the plea to her mother had not been fulfilled when she was a little girl and certainly could not be gratified today. She decided to give up this unrealistic demand she had been making for years.

Coming to terms with her demand upon her mother required awareness on an emotional level and a deliberate Adult decision to change. Of course, the problem will recur because of her old conditioned way of responding to her needs. Yet, each time, she will be aware of the hidden message 'I want love' more easily and more quickly and will be able to institute new behaviour in her relationship with her mother and other mother-figures.

Bringing the past into the present via the magic of the 'empty chair' changes a useless recounting of past information with the usual excuses and explanations (called chickenshit, bullshit and elephantshit by Dr Perls) into an emotionally charged encounter. The emotions are the perceptual level on which effective psychotherapy occurs – the necessary fuel for personality growth.

The Rubber band effect

A married woman being treated for depression finally became aware of the anger in her cry. Her boiler full of hostile feelings then erupted and almost daily she had inappropriate outbursts of shrieking rage directed towards her children and her husband. While her anger no longer produced depression, she was quite disturbed by the intensity and the scapegoating effects of her rage. As group therapy progressed, I asked her to open up her anger through various encounter techniques, and she exploded until we all began to hear her 'shriek'. At that moment, she heard within herself the scream of a frightened little girl. She then transformed her shriek into words: 'Listen to me, listen to me.' It had been a silent scream buried within a five-year-old girl who could not yell for the attention and affection she needed. And thus she had remained emotionally hungry and alone. This was a rubber band effect. By opening up her anger, here now, she had released a shriek that was connected by a 'rubber band' with the little girl in the past. The little girl was still there in the adult woman, and was still afraid to ask for affection, since today this action might be misinterpreted sexually.

As she experienced the little girl within her, she also recalled the favourite and most frightening story of her childhood: *Alice in Wonderland*. She remembered that when Alice screamed with anger the Queen yelled 'Off with her head,' and that the next picture in her book was of all the cards falling in upon Alice. Of course, the story *Alice in Wonderland* only symbolized the 'Don't be angry' message that her parents had instilled in her. This was why she could not scream as a child. But she now realized, as Alice did in the story, that the cards were only cards and that being angry was not as dangerous as she had thought it was when she was a little girl.

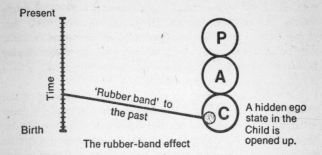

The rubber-band effect

The opening up of new ego states, that is, roles that have been submerged or disowned, seems to have a rubber band effect with the past, and reveals unsolved emotional conflicts and relationships that have persisted from the past into the present in a hidden way. The patient described above brought into awareness a part of herself, a lonely little girl who screamed silently. With this new emotional insight she could deal more effectively and directly with her need for affection and reduce the anger of her frustrations.

14 Feeling your anger

Men don't cry

Many of us look upon the display of feelings as a sign of weakness, instability and immaturity. Men must 'play it cool', 'keep a stiff upper lip' and 'be tough'. They must approach a crisis without flinching and respond to a tragedy, a death or a loss without visible pain. Society's code usually does not allow men to express love and affection without being labelled effeminate. As a result, their sexual behaviour may be reduced to a display of silent efficiency, the physical act being completed with a minimum of talking and emotion.

Effective psychotherapy requires work and perception on the level of emotions. But many men and women suppress their feelings. They rely heavily on the Adult computer and live by the Parent slogan, 'Men (and women) don't cry.' They deny the feelings that are needed to explore the Child ego state and to open their anger. Their 'cry', strangely enough, may be a depression, and the feelings of sadness, inadequacy and failure may be a defence against the anger within.

Fortunately, many people today have scrapped the old record of 'Don't feel' and have become warmly natural and spontaneous, with a rich flow of feelings, a sense of aliveness and an involvement in living now. They show their emotions as a true expression of trust and intimacy with others. Of course, there are problems in the liberation of feelings and the relaxing of controls. Excesses may lead to violence, sexual abuse and promiscuity; new problems will arise that will require new solutions. Yet, the expression of feelings is necessary for the resolution of emotional conflicts. The vigorous and explosive expression of emotion is frequently labelled a 'breakdown', yet many times I have found it to be a 'breakthrough' and a part of the process of 'breaking free'.

The experience of anger

A compulsive woman suffered a depression following her husband's death. She knew intellectually that her sadness contained anger – anger at him for drinking himself to death while still in his early forties. A year later she suffered an 'anniversary reaction', a flare-up of depression with a return of memories and feelings about her husband's death. She kept visualizing him in his terminal coma and she cried continually. The pain of her sadness was so unbearable that she wanted to die. I considered her suicidal impulses to be dangerous and arranged for her to be hospitalized.

The hospital routine, the accommodation and the attitudes of the staff so infuriated her that she began to vent her anger and demanded release. She repeatedly expressed her rage, and within a few days was feeling better and could be discharged. Feeling and expressing her rage, even in a scapegoating way, produced recovery. As her anger receded, she recognized that her thoughts over her husband's death no longer produced tears. She had completed her mourning in response to the 'anniversary reaction'.

In my early days of using the newer techniques, I had an interesting but somewhat frightening experience with a young woman I will call Martha. Then in her early thirties, Martha had for many years been suffering recurrent depression. Some of these episodes required hospitalization. She had been with me for about a year in group therapy and her progress had not been satisfactory; in fact, it had been minimal.

One day she told us about an upsetting encounter that morning with her boss. I asked her to imagine her boss in the 'empty chair' and to talk to him in the present. She immediately became angry and said, 'You are like my father.' I then asked her to put her father in the 'empty chair' and talk to him. Within a minute, she exploded with intense rage towards her father. She went wild with anger, put her head down and charged at me. Her angry Child was completely out of control, and I was forced to wrestle with her on the floor to prevent her from hurting herself or me. The blind screaming rage lasted for what seemed like an eternity but was probably only about ten minutes.

While I held Martha on the floor, fantasies went through my mind. I could see her hospitalized again for a psychotic rage attack, and my new techniques blamed for her illness. I could imagine headlines in the paper saying 'Psychiatrist Drives Woman Crazy'. Finally Martha settled down, and after the meeting she drove home. I went home myself, but even after I had eaten dinner I was concerned and worried about her. So I returned to my office, took out her chart and telephoned her home. Her husband answered, and I asked in a somewhat subdued voice, 'Is Martha OK?' He responded quite excitedly, 'She has just told me about the wonderful experience she had in therapy today!' I had been frantically worrying over Martha's explosion, while she and her husband considered it a therapeutic breakthrough. Surprisingly enough, after that encounter Martha progressed quickly and became more assertive in her marriage. Her husband, who had frequently been in a domineering Parent role, treating her like a little girl, was brought to terms quite openly by her. As they readjusted their relationship, Martha worked out her conflicts and in a few months terminated therapy, well adjusted. About a year later, she called me to tell me that she was moving to another province, and that she was still healthy and essentially free from any disabling bouts of depression.

Expressing anger – sometimes irrationally, sometimes unjustly – has a therapeutic effect in itself. The anger may then be used to change a relationship or to relieve an 'anniversary' depressive reaction.

15 Reowning your anger

When you recognize that 'the anger I see is me' (p 15), that you have denied most of your own hostility and have projected it on others, you will have made a difficult and important discovery. It may be painful at first, for you may go from the projection or paranoid position to the depressed one. You may be so flooded with hostility that you turn it inwards, in a guilty or self-blaming way. However, sadness is healthier and is in the direction of growth and recovery, for the next step is to accept, utilize and dispose of your anger.

Jan was a Jew. In his job he felt persecuted because of his religion and ostracized by his fellow workers. He found himself ignored and rejected at work. 'What is the matter with other people that they are filled with hate and anti-Semitism?' he asked himself. He was a kind, gentle person who offended no one so how could they react to him with such hostility? He told his story to his family doctor, who recommended psychiatric consultation. Jan agreed, but was perplexed. He felt that nothing was wrong with him, that the problem existed in others.

Jan was a survivor of a concentration camp. As a boy he had seen indescribable cruelty and terror. He had watched his mother being marched nude to the gas chamber. He had seen bodies piled high in mountains of death. But what had the past to do with the present? What was still alive that impaired his daily life? The answer was guilt, his guilt over survival and over his rejection of the Jewishness that had brought him such terrible suffering. This guilt persisted in every encounter and required the atonement of suffering. In therapy, he became aware of his guilt and suffering, and, as he felt and experienced it, he also began to experience his underlying anger. He felt anger towards the past – towards the Nazis, towards God and towards a critical father. He felt anger in the present towards the fears and relationships of daily life. He was angry that he had totally masked his personality by an 'armour' of niceness. As he reowned his hostility, he recognized the pleasure he felt at his aggressiveness. His pseudomutuality (the phony cloak of gentleness, kindness and passivity) disappeared. He became alive and assertive. Some of his co-workers resented his happiness; some of his friends withdrew from him, finding him coarse and arrogant. But he did not care; he did not even see these rejections as anti-Semitism. Other people actively sought his company and made approaches of warmth and friendliness. His social life expanded and he enjoyed new, intimate sexual relationships. He was amazed at how the intensity of anti-Semitism seemed to decrease as he reowned his own hostility.

To find out whether you are projecting, fantasize in a personal way the anger you see. Feel some of the hostility. Try the anger on, and, if it fits, reown it and take the risk of using it in a way that is 'you'.

16 Lowering your hostility

Change your critical Parent

You can decrease your anger production by lowering the demands of your critical, perfectionistic Parent ego state. Listen to the idealistic, unrealistic demands for achievement made by your Parent. Become aware of the continuous 'shoulds' and 'musts'. Allow the Child within you to say 'No' or 'I won't' to the excessive pressure. Help your Adult and Child to make decisions on wants and desires, based on your own individuality. Some people respond to suggestions like these with 'I'll run wild,' or 'Maybe I'll rape and plunder.' All I can say in answer is that, if your Child wants to explode, you can always use your Adult to guide it. If you re-educate the Parent ego state, you can reduce many of the angry interactions, internal and external, that result from its demands, and, most important, you will prevent the occurrence of self-blaming depressions.

If you want to lower your anger towards others, you can accomplish this simply by decreasing your Parental demands and expectations. If you 'hear' the arrogant, condescending, critical Parent in your head, condemning you and belittling others, remember that you have the power to stop it.

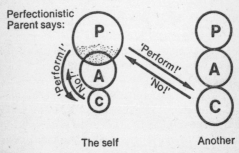

Perfectionistic Parent says:

The self   Another

Lower your expectations — say no!

Resolve your dependency needs

One of the best ways to reduce excess anger is to resolve hostile-dependent relationships. The basic angry-Child-to-Parent interactions are disguised in many life settings – at work, home and school, and in society. The way you meet basic needs for love and recognition determines your emotional health or illness.

For many years, a young woman had suffered intense periods of crying, depression, anxiety and fear. Periodically, she exploded. Sometimes her moods changed dramatically, from euphoria at one moment to intense sadness and suicidal impulses at the next. She was emotionally unstable and her psychiatric label was 'hysterical personality disorder'. She spent most of her time daydreaming and had frequent sexual fantasies with a painful or suffering theme. Her main period of emotional upheaval began with the loss of a lover. Although it was years earlier, she still mourned for him almost daily.

Her course in group therapy was dramatic and explosive, yet without much progress; and her behaviour in the group characterized her major underlying problem in living. During the first year of therapy she became more and more upset with each meeting. She disliked the group and recognized that she wanted my attention, even admitting to sexual fantasies about me. Her tension level in the group was extreme; she frequently cried, shook and was aware of intense fear without cause. She constantly asked 'Why, why, why?' and made emotional appeals to me for help, often calling me after hours, always in acute distress and suicidal. Yet any approach by me seemed to fail. While she begged for help, she resisted any rescue attempt I made. It was really a year-long game of Why Don't You – Yes But (p 101); the completely discouraged patient appealed to me, her therapist, for miracles, yet angrily and unconsciously rejected any approach I made.

Then one day she made a sudden and unexpected appearance at my office, demanding to see me. She had something important to say. At first she cried and shook, as she always did; then she finally burst out, 'Damn you, why don't you help me! You're a psychiatrist, so make me better!' Her anger was mixed with anxiety and tearfulness. She continued to explode and kept repeating, 'Damn you, make me better. Why don't you help me?' I responded, 'I am helping you, as much as I can.' She finally ran out of the office, yelling and slamming the door.

Her core, the hostile-dependent problem, was bare at last. Her hungry, demanding Child wanted a magical Parent to cure her. She was Waiting for Santa Claus, and angry as hell because he was not there. At this point growth could begin. She could come to terms on a different level with the demands she was making on me and other people. She could give up the search for the omnipotent Parent and assume responsibility for herself. She could go out and get her needs met, rather than waiting for deliverance. She could take a chance on herself, and emerge on a level of self-reliant living. Or, on the other hand, she could quit therapy and look for a new psychiatrist, a new lover, or a new boss who would be the perfect Parent. She was at a crossroads of emotional awareness and pain that required the decision for change. If she chose to turn at that moment to a different way of relating to people, to an Adult heterosexual level of functioning, her demands on others would decrease, and so would her angry feelings. The decrease in her hostility would be dramatically reflected in all phases of living, and would result in the loss of anxiety and depression.

Use your Adult ego

Marked emotional upheaval is constantly present when you have a formidable, critical Parent ego state and an angry, demanding Child reacting together in the framework of your personality. The two continually produce great amounts of anger within and without.

One nervous and emotionally unstable young woman shook as she described her 'only' incapacitating problem: severe insomnia. While she was describing this difficulty, her voice and hands trembled, her body perspired and her eyes filled with tears. As she realized that two opposite parts of her personality were causing her dilemma, her level of excitement rose to near the explosion point. I asked her to place each part of her personality in a chair and have a spontaneous dialogue between them. Her body noticeably shaking, she soon became immersed in the dialogue of screaming rage between her ego states. One part insisted, 'You should sleep, you stupid bitch!' (critical Parent) and the other part cried, 'Get off my back!' (angry Child). This constant intra-personal battle had resulted in a personality that bristled with rage, overproduced hostility in a vicious, circular manner, was always ready to explode and was too tense to sleep.

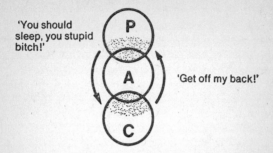

Whenever this woman had an important crisis in her life, the internal struggle between her critical Parent and her angry Child would result in the overproduction of hostility, creating one hell of an angry woman. In transactions with other people, her angry Child or critical Parent would contaminate her Adult by sneaking in to disrupt relationships. Soon it became easy for her to recognize and separate the angry Child, but it was very difficult for her to detect the critical Parent, whom she frequently mistook for the factual, sensible Adult. Gradually she realized that the critical Parent was her mother's 'voice' in her head. Using this insight, she was gradually able to end her internal turmoil and external conflicts by bringing in her uncontaminated Adult. The recognition, separation and maturation of her Adult ego state was necessary for tranquillity, stability and peaceful relations with others.

'Where it's at'

One communication pattern for lowering your anger involves finding out where the other person is 'at'. For example, if you are talking through your Adult, in an attempt to reach the other person's Adult, and he responds with his angry Child or critical Parent, you recognize that your communication is crossed and that he is not available now to receive your information. Of course, the more you try to reach him at this point the angrier you become. If instead you recognize where he is 'at' – what ego state he is in – you may be able to stop the interaction and explain the communication problem, thereby giving him an oppor-

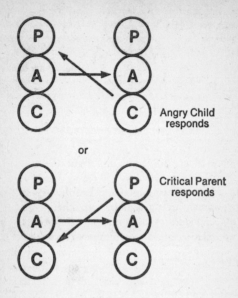

Angry Child
responds

or

Critical Parent
responds

Crossed communication

tunity to gain self-awareness and switch his ego state. As a psychiatrist, I occasionally hook the angry Child of a person who sees me as a critical Parent. At that moment I take pains to have him see me as I really am, a logical Adult. If he cannot do so, I reduce my own hostility level by ending the transaction at that point, and return to it at a later date. The technique of checking where another person is 'at' in an interaction certainly keeps my boiler of angry feelings reduced.

In any relationship between you and me, if each of us recognizes where the other is at, and if neither of us becomes a rescuer, a persecutor, or a victim, then I am OK and you are

OK. Our relationship will then be free of manipulative and destructive games, and without the painful, emotional symptoms of anxiety or depression. A minimum of anger will be generated between us, and any anger that is produced will be dealt with quickly and efficiently in an adaptive manner that does not destroy closeness.

Giving up old resentments

A young married man who came to me for treatment spoke like a computer, giving me the facts without much warmth or emotional involvement. Then, during a touch encounter in which his face was touched and he was spoken to as a loving parent might talk to a child, he burst into tears. He began to relive his life at the time his mother had committed suicide. A flood of hidden emotions burst forth, revealing his intense sadness and his marked resentment towards her for killing herself. Only after this ventilation subsided was he able to forgive her and close the chapter that had remained incomplete for many years, repressed but unsolved. From that time on, it was as if the energy that he needed to hide his feelings was available for constructive purposes. He grew emotionally and became a feeling, responsive human being. Not only was he in touch with himself, but he was warm and responsive to others.

Another married man in his early thirties was telling me how extremely angry he was at his 'crazy mother', who had brought him up almost in isolation. She was an extremely obsessional woman who not only prevented him from playing with other children but insisted on immaculate cleanliness. He openly hated her; and when I asked how long he was going to hate her, he said, 'The rest of my life'.

Why he was going to carry this intense hatred he did not know; but he did know that he was not going to put it down till the day he died. In any situation that this man approached, his boiler of angry feelings was already three-quarters full, and any little addition brought him close to rage attacks. He knew that this was interfering with his work and impairing his social relationships. How could he lower his resentments? How could he lower his hostility to a tolerable level? Of course, the answer

143

was to give up his old anger towards his mother – the old grudge that was extremely painful and kept old wounds open.

Many times he tried in therapy to resolve his hate towards his mother. Yet, as he spoke to her in the 'empty chair' and attempted to forgive her, he could always hear the anger in his words and recognized that he still hated her. He was not prepared to forgive her for her past or relate to her in a new way in the present. If he could succeed in closing the chapter of his past resentments, he would then be able to see her today as she really was. He might still decide that he did not like her as a person, but the intensity of past hate, the boiler of old anger, the old childhood blame felt towards her, would be gone. And, if he could dispose of his old hostilities towards his mother, he would no longer scapegoat other women, upon whom he put his mother's face.

Stop scapegoating

Scapegoating gives only temporary relief to our anger and rarely solves the problems that produced it in the first place. A major way to reduce our hostility is to recognize our scapegoating and deal with the anger in the relationship in which it belongs.

One woman in psychotherapy began to experience intense, continuous and totally inappropriate hostility to her husband, which flared up at the least provocation. In a 'hot seat' encounter I asked her to imagine her husband in the 'empty chair' and to blast away at him. She soon let forth a torrent of angry expression towards her husband. At that moment I asked her to imagine another face on her husband in the 'empty chair'. Immediately, tears came to her eyes and her anger dissipated as she recognized the image of her long-dead father. Tearfully she ventilated her anger at her father for his total rejection of her while she was growing up. He had been a quiet and withdrawn man who rarely stroked her. At that moment she recognized that she had been putting her father's face symbolically on her husband, blaming him for her father's rejection and demanding from him a father's acceptance of a daughter. With the emotional awareness of her scapegoating, she was able to look clearly at her husband as a totally unique individual, separate from the unresolved relationship with her father, and subsequently she lowered her hostility.

Another woman recognized that she scapegoated by putting her mother's face on her husband and constantly played the role of 'a good little girl' to him, seeking his approval. She was playing an old childhood script of seeking her mother's affection and being angry when she did not get it.

The next time you find yourself scapegoating and blowing your boiler of angry feelings inappropriately, try the technique of 'putting another face' on the person involved, to find out who you are really angry at. The pay-off may be a reduction in your hostility and more appropriate and realistic interpersonal relationships.

Give up your racket

Eric Berne used the word 'racket' to describe the self-indulgence of bad feelings such as guilt, fear, depression and anger. I only use this word with caution, in talking with my patients, because it has a belittling connotation and seems to ignore the possibility of genuine suffering. However, I have seen a number of patients who have learned to indulge in bad feelings as a way of getting (negative) strokes, and they picked up the habit from the way they were treated by their parents, who paid greatest attention to their children's expressions of unpleasant feelings, such as sadness and anger. I had a patient who clung to a racket of depression; she was afraid of physical closeness and, rather than facing this problem and trying to resolve it, she used her racket as a way of hooking her husband's attention. Another of my patients, a man with an angry racket, summed up his attitude by saying, 'When I yell, it's the only time people will listen to me.'

If you think that you may be working a racket, reflect on your past and try to recognize feelings you experienced in your childhood that are still active within you today. If you find that you have, for example, an angry racket, you can make the decision to give it up, and set yourself free to offer and receive positive strokes of love, warmth, trust and caring, for yourself and for others.

145

17 Accepting your anger

'I hate my children!'

Would you be surprised if I said that many parents, especially mothers, do not admit or accept the idea that at certain times they hate their children? Let us look at this objectively. Young children are frequently in their demanding Child ego state, yelling, 'Give it to me,' and 'Me too, me too.' This easily hooks the anger of parents, especially mothers. Why mothers? Simply because, most of the time, they are at home with their children. While mothers can accept the love they feel towards their children, many of them have a great deal of trouble accepting the anger they feel.

I do not think I have seen as much guilt in any other relationship as that which can build up in angry parents as they sense some of the negative feelings they have about their own children. Some women say it is OK to be angry at children, but feel that they overact and that their feelings are inappropriate. There is no doubt that children are the easiest people to scapegoat. The build-up of hostility that you feel towards adults can often be triggered by a trivial incident involving a young child. I think that violent attacks on children are frequently due to the 'boiler theory' of repression of angry feelings. I also feel that many women who have rage attacks are really unable to accept their anger and to release it in any effective way. They are frightened of its harm or its dangers, so they push it deep down in their boiler, where it builds up until it explodes. Of course, when it explodes, the violence they see only proves to them that their anger is unacceptable. This leads to a vicious circle of repression and subsequent feelings of emotional discomfort, punctuated by rage explosions. The guilt I have seen in mothers over their hostility to their children is almost unbelievable. I have seen women plagued by their impulses towards their children. The conflict between their affection and their hostility has precipitated many depressions and some suicides.

The secret, once again, is to accept your feelings from moment to moment, to use them and deal with them so as to solve problems and avoid both extremes of anger – the depression at one end and the build-up to rage explosions at the other when the boiler bursts. The next time you feel guilty about your hostility towards your children, remember that they are unique individuals with their own ego states and a natural drive for survival. Even at a young age they have Parent, Adult and Child ego states that give them a choice and a flexibility of behaviour for healthy development. Sure, you want to be a good parent; but remember that children can grow up healthily because they have individuality and can learn to be responsible for themselves.

Family fighting
How many times do you hear parents say to each other, 'We shouldn't fight in front of the children'? I believe this is a mistake in family rearing. Children learn mostly by copying. How are they going to learn to argue and express their resentments effectively if you, as a parent, do not help them? How are they going to learn that it is OK to be angry if you, by your avoidance, spread the message that anger is bad, harmful or dangerous? I think it is OK to be angry in front of your children, so that they too can learn to handle this emotion. There is a pleasure that parents can experience in fighting with their children. I personally find if very satisfying when I can argue and yell at my children and they can express their resentments back. In this way we close the incident, dissipate our hostility and can carry on with the next part of living.

Anger at sickness
If you are a parent, how many nights have you spent awake tending a sick child? I am sure many parents have had this experience and are fully aware of the sympathy, the compassion and the concern they expended. But I wonder how many would admit with equal ease the resentment and the hostility they felt towards the illness itself, and even towards the child for being sick. How often can we express or even accept our anger at the stress or anxiety caused by a sick child?

Obnoxious children

I cannot leave the area of anger towards children without talking about the negatively stroked child. This is the obnoxious child who seems always able to hook your criticisms, your anger, your resentments and your negative attention. There is often one child in a family who seems to grow only when he is kicked. We might guess why this happens. Maybe he is one of a large family, and the only way he can get attention is through unpleasantness and misbehaviour. Nevertheless, this child is constantly getting his emotional strokes in a negative form of recognition. He even seems to go out of his way to get this. He appears to have an amazing ability to turn any pleasurable event into disruption, in order to get negative attention. He seems to work on the principle that a kick is better than no attention at all.

I would like to suggest how to handle this kind of child, but with a warning that it is not a foolproof method. The important thing is not to feel guilty. Do not kick yourself for responding the way you do to this child, because his ability to hook your criticism is of almost professional quality. You might ignore, as much as possible, his misbehaviour and the opportunities he creates for negative stroking. You might respond only when you genuinely feel like doing so in a positive way. You might also make it a point to recognize him for good behaviour, or even for just being. Stroke him positively as much as you can. It is a difficult job and quite a challenge. I believe that persistence and recognition in a positive way may, in time, change a child's conditioning from negative forms of loving to positive forms of loving. Children who are negatively conditioned usually grow up playing games that have unpleasant 'pay-offs' of negative feelings and 'loser' scripts.

Don't kick yourself

Through the use of the Parent, Adult and Child concepts of personality, I get a clearer understanding of how opposite feelings, such as love and hate, can coexist in a person. The psychiatric term for this is 'ambivalence', the existence of opposite feelings in day-to-day rel ionships. For example, sometimes while playing squash I will recognize that my opponent has made an extremely good shot. The Parent in me might say 'Good shot' (a 'should'), but I sense that my Child ego state is angry at being defeated. This mixture of positive and negative feelings exists in most of us. Yet the love-and-hate feelings may be difficult to tolerate. If your negative feelings seem out of keeping with the situation, you may kick yourself for being angry. But with your awareness of the different attitudes of Parent, Adult and Child ego states you can accept without self-blame conflicting ideas and feelings that you have about life. So, if your angry Child seems incompatible with the ideas of your logical Adult, do not bring in your critical Parent to administer punishment. Allow for the coexistence of opposites.

Even if you make mistakes or have accidents, do not kick yourself; do not turn your hostility inwards. Hear the voice of the critical Parent in your head, and stop the onslaught of self-torture. If you make a mistake, then bring in your Adult to correct it, or your loving Parent ego state to nurture the Child within you.

The Kick Me game, like other psychological games, is unconscious; but, by turning in on yourself, you can become aware of the three parts within you and control your response. There is intense pleasure and satisfaction in knowing yourself, controlling your response, widening your freedom of choice of behaviour and increasing your independence.

As I stated earlier, the self-punitive game of Kick Me may be a method of fulfilling your life script. If you have a 'loser' script like 'Be a failure,' 'Don't grow up,' 'Don't be you,' 'Die,' 'Self-destruct,' 'Suffer,' or 'Commit suicide,' the game of Kick Me is only a means to an end. Getting in touch with your script may require professional help, although you may be able to recognize your life theme by concentrating on the message or 'moral' of your favourite story. For example, I discovered one of my life scripts through the story 'Horton the Elephant' by Dr Seuss; by hatching an elephant bird, Horton finally got his reward for hard work and perseverance. You might also find your life script by fantasizing your future in the next two, three or four years, or by imagining that you are wearing a sweat shirt with inscriptions you have chosen on the front and back.

149

Writing your own epitaph might also help you to clarify your life's goals. Getting in touch with your 'first act' – your first childhood recollections, either fantasy or real, that appear related to your present problem – can bring to awareness the life script by which you live today.

A certain married actress had, essentially, a life plan of 'Don't be angry.' As a result, she usually reacted verbally with the opposite of anger – whith phony words of obsequiousness clothed in false smiles. Yet her angry Child could not be submerged completely and would often sneak out in devious ways beyond her awareness. She acted out much of her anger towards her husband by frigidity and extra-marital affairs. Frequently she suffered from Kick Me depression (anger-in). Sometimes the anger almost burst into awareness as she manipulated others with pleasant words. Often she scapegoated her children with rage that belonged to others.

In group therapy she became acutely aware of the way she spoke. She recognized the extreme softness of her voice, the gentleness and niceness of her words. With this revelation, she recalled a childhood picture of her 'mother's big mouth yelling terrible words' and recalled making a decision at that time not to be like her mother. Her neurosis was the result of a childhood memory of disgust at and rejection of her mother's anger – a child's picture of a mother that affects the adult living today. With her present insights she has made a new decision, a new script – 'to be angry' and to use her anger in direct confrontation and problem-solving.

Making new decisions about old life scripts will help you to find other ways of living without the game of Kick Me. Remember, however, that there is a risk. For example, you may have to experiment with directing your anger outwards, where it really belongs. Are you ready to take a chance?

Of course, you may think that anger-out is blaming others, but I see it as a reaction to frustration – an expression of the self, a reowning of the 'I', and an assertive acceptance of personal responsibility, without blaming others for your predicament. Rather than saying 'You make me angry,' you would say, 'I am angry at you.'

One destructive form of anger-out is Now I've Got You, You Son of a Bitch. It is really 'hitting below the belt', and will only prolong angry interactions. So when NIGYSOB erupts, put a time limit on it. Three to five minutes of blowing your top should be sufficient, then stop it! Take a chance to grow by accepting full responsibility for your anger and confronting the person involved. While it is tempting to 'get the bastard', if you keep to the area of conflict your back-and-forth dialogue may resolve your anger and close the issue (complete the Gestalt).

18 Showing your anger

Show me your hostility Here and Now – 'how'

I am not suggesting that the way to emotional stability is to have diarrhoea of angry feelings. I doubt very much that the continual venting of your hostility would bring you peace and contentment, let alone social acceptance. However, I do believe that any overload of resentment that you have built up over the years and that periodically erupts can be disposed of. You may need professional help to become aware of and experience your 'old angry recordings', and to relegate them once and for all to the archives. Dr Perls feels that we have many incomplete chapters, or incomplete Gestalts, that need to be ended and put away, if we are to get on with living in the present.

Deal with the daily frustrations and irritations of living in a direct and natural way. Ventilate your hostilities here and now, as they develop, in a socially acceptable manner. Allow your angry Child out, under the supervision of your Adult. Let your voice express your resentment. If your critical Parent comes in to punish you for your hostility, stop it. You do not have to justify your angry Kid, but you do need to accept it and guide it to solve the problems of living. Occasionally, you may have to swallow your rage. If you cannot actually ventilate your anger, you can fantasize doing so. Put the person who irritates you in the 'empty chair' and talk to him. You may need to sublimate your hostility and to express it in indirect ways that give relief; for example, physical activities, sports, play and work are all excellent ways of working off resentments and frustrations. Many of us can vicariously relieve our hostility through spectator sports, or entertainment or movies dealing with aggression or violence. There are other safe antidotes. For example, I like to spend my noon hour at the local 'Y', ventilating and sublimating my aggressions and hostility through such vigorous exercises as karate, squash and swimming.

Basically, the anger within us can be sensed through one of two ego states: the angry Child and the critical Parent. The

Adult plays a part by allowing and guiding the anger rather than censoring or repressing it.

'You' and your hostility

It is common to talk about yourself, 'I', by using the second-person pronoun, 'you'. I do not think it is a matter of language usage at all; the use of 'you' meaning 'I' is really a clue to the voice of your Parent ego state. It may even be a direct quote from your parents or authorities in the past. If we listen closely to these parental injunctions, we can hear old guidelines – 'shoulds' and 'musts' – on how to handle anger, old prescriptions that may need rewriting for today's living. Here are some I have heard from my patients: 'You just don't talk back.' 'When you lose your temper people go away from you, they think you're loony.' 'You should be seen and not heard.' 'You shouldn't be angry, you should be nice.' 'You're weak if you show your feelings.'

Listen for the 'you' in conversation and recognize in it the Parent ego state. The parental statements from the past may

Parent, Adult, and Child ego states within the Child

coincide with the Child's life scripts or decisions about anger,* such as, 'I won't be angry.' When this happens, bring in your Adult ego state to make new decisions as to how, when, and

* On a level of secondary Transactional Analysis the 'you' statement may be occurring within the Parent ego state that lies within the Child ego state – actually within the adaptive Child.

where you will use your hostility. As you talk about your anger, use the pronoun 'I'. By assuming personal responsibility, you strengthen your personal identity.

Getting in touch with your hostility

Most of us, as we experience unpleasant symptoms of anxiety or depression, try to avoid them as much as possible. If we are anxious in a crowd, we withdraw. If we are depressed, we try to do something to help us forget it. The next time you become emotionally uncomfortable, feel it, 'stay with it' and become aware of your total self in the present. Explore yourself, not on a logical level but on an experiential level. Listen to your body and become aware of yourself as a total feeling human being in the present. You may find that during an anxiety attack you hold your breath, and that simply by regular deep breathing you can alleviate the tension. You may even want to sigh and make sounds, as one patient did who mumbled and then finally said the word 'shit', in this way ventilating his hostility and relieving his anxiety.

Tune in to your ego states – 'listen to the voices in your head', feel the many people within you. You could try a dialogue with yourself and attempt to get in touch with hidden parts. Talk to your depression and allow it to answer back, while keeping in touch with your body's response and the tone and quality of your voice. You can even fantasize to get in touch with your emotions, using the words 'Now I am aware' to reach your feelings. This technique of experiential self-awareness may be difficult, but perseverance usually brings success. It is a new way of perceiving yourself and attempting to come to terms with your emotional difficulty. It is really 'getting in touch with your hostility' on the level of feeling rather than on the intellectual level.

I was very moved by an experience I had with a young mother. She told us that she was becoming aware of her hostility and was beginning to use it. In the process, however, she was scapegoating her ten-year-old son, who, unfortunately, reacted by withdrawal and crying. She recognized the injustice of her behaviour, yet found him so easy to attack. The following week she told us that he came home from school one day crying, and appeared very sad.

She asked, 'Why are you crying?'

He responded, 'The teacher was screaming today.'

'Was she screaming at you?' the mother asked.

'No,' he replied, 'she was screaming at all of us.'

Then the mother asked. 'What did you want to say to her?'

'I don't know,' he answered.

'Why don't you close your eyes and pretend you're back in school,' his mother suggested. 'What do you feel like saying to your teacher?'

The son yelled out, 'Fuck you!'

His mother then said, 'I guess you get pretty angry when the teacher screams, and that is OK. And you know it is even OK to be angry at me when I scream at you. It really is OK to be angry back.'

The son broke into tears and ran into his mother's arms. They were tears of relief and pleasure and he said, 'OK.' What a beautiful start to helping her young son get in touch with his hostility and handle it in a problem-solving and pleasurable way!

Listening

Most of us can hear but we do not always listen. Listening is more than the semi-automatic awareness of sound; it is an intellectual and emotional focus on the communication of others. You can also listen to your own voice and in this way get in touch with your anger.

Many of my patients, in the process of solving their problems, use the word 'can't'. They say, 'I can't give up my marriage and my children.' 'I can't be happy,' or 'I can't do my work.' By the word 'can't' they usually mean that they think it is impossible and beyond their personal control. When they substitute 'won't' for 'can't', exciting things can happen. First, they have taken personal responsibility for their actions. Second, by listening to the word 'won't', repeating it, exaggerating it, and saying it louder and louder, they can become aware of the angry Child within them. Then they can use their hostility for emotionally healthy living.

A post-graduate university student kept saying, 'I can't complete my doctoral thesis.' Daily, he would make plans to work, but then he usually found some interference. On days when he sat down at his desk, he found that he couldn't (wouldn't?) concentrate. One day, as he was thinking about his thesis, saying 'can't', he changed the word to 'won't', as had been suggested in group therapy. Suddenly he heard, felt and visualized his angry Child screaming, 'I won't do it!' He became excited and laughed as he enjoyed this new emotional awareness of his defiance. He then brought in his Adult to make a new decision: that he was not ready to complete his thesis at this time, and would leave university for a year. His new plans for living took into account the feelings of his angry Child, and he knew that he would return when he wanted to complete his degree.

The word 'but' often indicates a switch in ego states. It frequently denies everything that has just been said; for example, 'I love my wife but . . .' Sometimes 'but' is the word that exposes the activities of the shit-disturbing, mischievous, defiant Child, which has been trying to nullify every positive suggestion. A tilting of the head or a subtle smile often accompanies the 'but' of the angry Child ego state.

As you listen to and observe yourself, try to pick up the signals that you use when you change ego states. The clue may be a little cough, a change of voice, a gesture or a grimace.

Getting in touch with your hostility through encounter techniques

Say 'No'
How often do you have the pleasure of saying no? Getting in touch with your 'no', yelling it, screaming it, ventilating it, may help you to become aware of yourself. As you sense the anger, you may feel some resistance to it. Possibly you will shake with the intensity of your rage. Maybe you will be frightened and nervous, and possibly you will cry.

One young girl, in attempting to scream her 'no', thought she was yelling so loudly that she could be heard around the block. Would you believe that her voice was raised just a little above the conversational level? It was amazing; she really thought she was screaming her head off.

I suggest that you let out your 'no' somewhere in privacy to avoid embarrassment such as I once felt. I was swimming at the 'Y' when a colleague in the pool asked me to help him with a simple experiment. He went underwater and yelled his 'no', and then asked me if I could hear him. I could not, of course. He then said what a satisfying relief it was, and left the pool. As I swam I began to yell 'no' underwater, too, as loudly as I could. Suddenly I heard a voice yelling back at me. The lifeguard had run up to the side of the pool, ready to dive in and save me. I then realized that I had said my 'no' so enthusiastically that I had continued yelling even when I came up for breath. However, the best place to scream your 'no' is inside, against the 'shoulds' of your critical Parent.

Playing

While play can be a sublimation and a ventilation of hostility, sometimes it is a way to 'cry anger'. When we are able to sense, feel and recognize our anger, we can determine whether we are having difficulty in using or tolerating it.

One patient, an extremely quiet and passive young man, wanted to become more outgoing. I suggested a game of 'hand pushing', in which we stood about three feet apart and, with our hands, tried to push each other off balance. As we did this, he became aggressive and excited, his eyes twinkled, and he laughed. Quite suddenly he withdrew and put his head down. We discussed his behaviour and he recognized that while playing he had felt his angry, mischievous Child, and then had become frightened and anxious. He was consciously afraid of becoming violent, so he withdrew into passivity. Once he became aware of his character style of withdrawal as a defence against his potential violence, he was able to bring in his Adult to decide how to utilize his anger assertively. He recognized that, even if his Child had primitive, violent urges, he had an Adult that could harness this aggression, guide it, and use it creatively.

Bio-energetics

There are several techniques for encountering your anger. In one, two people oppose each other while yelling. One person says 'yes' and the other says 'no'; or one may yell 'Give it to me' while the other yells 'no'. Continuing this dialogue and raising your voice as loudly as you can will help you get in touch with hostility. Other techniques involve physical expression of anger. I have recently put hostility cushions into my office, and I encourage my patients to hit them with their fists, while breathing deeply, yelling their favourite and appropriate sound, and directing their feelings in fantasy towards people they resent. You can also kick a mattress while you are beating your hands, breathing deeply and yelling your hostility.

The above techniques are from the Bio-energetic concepts of Dr Alexander Lowen, who thought that keeping hostility locked in your body impaired the flow of normal emotional response. Getting in touch with hostility, even through such artificial means as yelling, can often help you to become conscious of a conflict, so that you may resolve it. Sometimes, expressing and ventilating rage may be sufficient to remove inhibitions and allow the continuation of emotional development.

In my practice I find that these hostility techniques produce various responses. Some people are so inhibited that they cannot do the exercises or allow themselves freedom of expression. Others do get in touch with their hostility. They even become aware of the cry behind the anger and hear the helpless, lonely Child that is looking for gratification of its needs. Getting in touch with this dependent Kid, feeling it, and accepting it may be sufficient for them to go on to a new level of emotional growth. Some patients feel relief as well as pleasure in the ventilation of their anger. Even getting in touch through artificial means sometimes brings to mind an awareness, allowing them to resolve angry conflicts, complete Gestalts and carry on in the present.

A bachelor was neurotically indecisive and ambivalent about marriage to his girlfriend. For years, they had planned to marry. Yet, as the day approached, he became intensely anxious and fearful, and cancelled the wedding.

We had previously discussed his problem of vacillation and

intellectually he recognized that it was a defence against anger and rage. I now asked him whether he wanted to open up his hostility emotionally, since intellectual awareness of it had accomplished nothing. When he agreed, I asked him to hit some cushions with a tennis racquet. I told him to hit as hard as possible, breathe deeply and make any sounds that he felt like making. Within a few minutes of vigorous effort, his whole body shook with rage. As he experienced his intense anger, he broke into a cry and fell to his knees. The words that came to his lips were, 'Momma, please love me.'

He began to describe his past life. The youngest of a large family, he had felt rejected and was treated as a weak, inadequate person. As he talked, he opened up unresolved areas in his Child ego state that pervaded his day-to-day living. He realized that his anger was only secondary to the frustration of his need for acceptance, love and self-esteem. Previously, he had intellectualized and rationalized his rage; now, experiencing it gave him a totally new perception and was extremely important for further personality work. He recognized that he had a life script of 'You're weak and inadequate, a failure' that affected everything he did and indirectly created his indecision about marriage. (PS They eloped.)

When we work through the Child ego state on the level of emotion response, problems emerge that seemingly have no logical connection with the obvious symptom. Yet what surfaces into conscious awareness may be the real problem that you must solve in order to rid yourself of emotional pain.

Cry anger

The words 'cry anger' have been used in different contexts throughout this book. At first they described the various cries of suffering, the distress of depression and the anxiety of perfectionism that mask underlying anger. Then they describe the dynamics of the Me Too, stroke-hungry Child that exists in all of us. We found that uncovering our anger sometimes revealed a lonely, emotionally starved Child, yelling for recognition and attention.

Now I would like to use the words 'cry anger' in what I think is their most important sense – to describe the scream of the angry Child ego state, the need to yell, to swear, to be the bastard or bitch that lies within. The angry Child can be coarse, vulgar, primitive, cruel, sadistic and even murderous. He can be spiteful, vengeful, mistrustful, jealous, bitter, hateful and violent. Periodically we must express the rage we feel in order to conquer and cure our emotional pain. We can avoid the extremes of the angry Child by venting our aggressions from moment to moment, as frustration occurs, to prevent the explosive build-up of rage and violence in our 'boilers'. In day-to-day living this ventilation of hostility may be gentle, but in an emotional crisis it may be intense and explosive. Our close relationships may have to endure repeated battles, perhaps for days, weeks or even months, before our rage is fully dissipated and the problems that produced it are solved. There is no other way: to cure our depression we must face our hostilities and 'cry anger'.

Anger should be like a mark upon water

One of the positive effects of anger is that, if used appropriately, it disappears like a mark made upon water. Expressing your resentments here and now in a human transaction allows the resolution of a communication problem and also the dissolution of your hostility. When the transaction is complete, you then get on with the new business of living. You may not believe this, but it can be exciting and satisfying to have an angry interchange with someone close to you. Instead of destroying the relationship, it can help you to grow together, to achieve greater pleasures and satisfactions from the relationship. I sincerely believe that the effective use of your hostility promotes personality growth.

When anger is like a mark upon water, it has become an effective problem-solving tool that completes Gestalts, closes chapters of your life and helps you enjoy the 'now' – the continuous living in the present without contamination from the past.

19 Living with anger

Decision-making – a risk

Insight alone, even on an experiential level, is not enough. One woman, with an awareness of her hostility, kept coming back without getting any relief from her depression. She was well aware of the intense anger she felt towards other people, but recognized that she still withdrew. As we explored this, we recognized some risks in her ventilating of hostility. She might become 'a bitch' or 'go crazy', or she might cry (as she often did when she was angry) and then become ashamed. She might lose control of her anger and become violent. She might be rejected by others because of her angry response, and lose a friend, a job or a spouse. People might think of her as overly emotional and lacking control, for in our society we praise 'keeping cool' in a crisis. One of her greatest fears about being angry was a fear of provoking physical retaliation, of being physically beaten by another person. It was a danger quite common in her childhood and it still haunted her today.

This woman had a decision to make: either to go into a depression, or to test out new patterns of behaviour and take the risks. She was faced not with acquiring more knowledge or insight, but with making a choice. In the past, she had chosen depression. Her job now was to learn how to do something different: what to do, and when and where to do it.

Assertiveness

Many people who are frightened of their hostility have violent fantasies in which they destroy others or are rejected. However, much to their surprise, when they finally begin to express themselves, they become genuine, assertive human beings. They are easily accepted by others, respond more spontaneously than ever before, and enjoy their self-assertion.

A young woman who always intellectualized about her behaviour and spoke in a soft voice gradually began to ventilate her hostility. One day she exclaimed, 'I have a voice, and it is great!' She became assertive, allowing her voice to carry her emotions of indignation and annoyance. She said, 'I don't swallow my anger any more.' Not only was there pleasure in her assertiveness, but her self-esteem went up as well, and she began to solve some of the difficulties in her relationships.

Many people have intellectual awareness of their hostility, yet fail to release it by letting their voices carry the emotion. They have made a decision like 'I won't show my feelings,' or 'I won't be angry'. One patient recalled that as a child she had hated her mother's hysterical outbursts but had decided not to show her feelings. As a result, even though she was aware of her serious marital conflict, she subdued her emotions. Of course, in a situation like this, the emotions usually seep through, bringing anxiety and depression. *The best tool in handling your emotions is the effective use of words and voice.*

I think assertiveness is the expression of anger, especially anger of the Child ego state under the guidance of the Adult ego

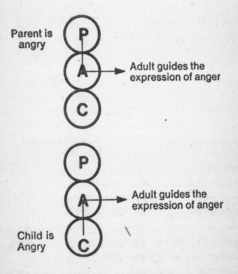

state. It may be, as well, the expression of the angry Parent projected through the eyes of the aware Adult. The Adult ego state decides how, when and where to express emotions; it evaluates the interactions of your ego states as well as your encounters with other people.

A young man in group therapy frequently played an active role as a co-therapist. One day, as he was playing Play Psychiatry, a sly smile crept across his face. As he experienced this smile, he recognized a mischievous and angry Child within him that wanted to create upheaval and trouble. He called it his 'shit-disturbing Kid'. He recognized that he had hidden it, and that he had an old 'Don't be angry' message from childhood. At this point, he made a decision to accept this part of himself and, as he did so, he became involved with people on a new level. He expressed himself openly and directly, and enjoyed the use of his anger; his personality widened with pleasure, laughter and fun. He made use of his different personality roles, and responded more flexibly to others. This, in time, affected many of his relationships; but, although he lost some old friends who resented his personality change, he was able to make new ones. He was no longer depressed, developed new interests and found life enjoyable and even exciting.

The OK Kid

Another young man stated that, when he was really in his angry 'shit-disturbing Kid' ego state, he was most confident and productive. It was a state in which he worked with real self-awareness and self-confidence – the point at which he felt most OK. His angry, cynical, sarcastic and aggressive self was a character he enjoyed – a part of himself that was exciting and alive. You, too, may find that expressing your anger raises your self-confidence to an OK level.

Anger can be caring

One woman told her group how she hated her mother-in-law and would really like to tell her to 'fuck off'. Of course, she could not do that, so she avoided contact with her mother-in-law, and withdrew into a depression when in her company. In the group, I asked this woman to imagine her mother-in-law in the 'empty chair' and tell her what she really felt. She said something like this: 'Since your husband died, you have really copped out. You have withdrawn into your shell. Now that you have the money and the freedom to go, why don't you take a trip to California, or Israel? Enjoy yourself and become involved in life again. If I can help you do it, I will be glad to.' The group was amazed as this woman 'told off' her mother-in-law; she had really burst forth with constructive anger – *anger that was caring and loving*. This is often the case – you become most angry at the people you love.

Anger can be intimate

A young man was intellectualizing about his problems and theorizing about his behaviour. Suddenly, he reacted angrily to my presence. He said he was irritated with me for just sitting there listening to him talk. As he voiced his irritation, he became anxious and tense. We explored the anxiety directly and openly, and he recognized that now he and I were communicating. He had used his anger to test the climate for intimacy, and yet he had a script that said that closeness was risky, that 'You can't trust anybody.'

An intimate relationship involves more than 'nice' things. It requires an ability to confront others directly with angry feelings. When married people say they never fight, I wonder whether they are able to genuinely love and be close. Of course, anger can be used to avoid closeness, especially when carried as a 'chip on the shoulder'. However, when used as assertive confrontation, anger can lead to intimacy.

Some people have described to me a 'rush', a 'high' without drugs, a 'peak' experience they have had. It is feeling of extreme pleasure and excitement that can occur in communication of intimacy. I have seen people cry with ecstasy as they relate the joy of genuine contact with another person – intimacy that can be produced by verbalizing anger.

Anger can be hateful

While I have stressed the positive side of anger and its use, I have omitted its destructive, unpleasant and disturbing aspects. I have done this mainly because I expect that the reader is only too familiar with the negative side – murder, war, racism, riots, crime. Yet I must discuss people who hate, who carry rage for years and years, who chronically feel hostile towards the world.

People who hate fall into a number of categories. There are those who feel 'I'm OK, you're not OK' and are always criticizing and condemning others. They are suspicious and feel persecuted. They usually deny their anger, projecting it on others. They admit their hostility only when they feel it is a justified response to attacks from others. Although they may not know it, their goal is to get rid of you.

Other people who hate are Ain't It Awful players, constantly whining and only too ready to show you their collection of past misfortunes. They continually blame others for their plight.

'I'm not OK, you're not OK' is mainly an attitude of the angry-Child ego state. Haters who feel this way reject themselves and the world and inflict violence and destruction on all, themselves included.

Some perfectionists are haters, and may be totally unaware of their chronic anger. They frequently play Now I've Got You, You Son of a Bitch and come across as rejecting, critical Parents or stubborn, defiant Children.

Most of the people who hate have a life style of suffering. As we strip away their masks, we uncover a Child angry at parental imperfection and waiting and holding on to his rage until the parents magically pay off – Waiting for Santa Claus.

The ecstasy of anger

The sexuality of aggression

It is my impression that many sexual crimes of rape, indecent assault and intercourse with violence or physical beating are interpreted wrongly as outbursts of sexual passion. I believe that the ecstasy comes from the expression of violence itself, and that the sexual assault is only a manifestation of the pathological aggression. The ecstasy of the hostility may also open up the thrill of sexuality and intensify the excitement. Even in normal sex, some of the excitement comes from the natural aggressiveness of the sexual act itself. It is important to recognize the presence of aggression in sadistic sex, for the key to prevention and treatment lies in understanding the psychology of abnormal hostility.

The ecstasy of violence

In the movies *A Clockwork Orange*, directed by Stanley Kubrick, and *Straw Dogs*, directed by Sam Peckinpaw, the ecstasy of aggression, anger and violence has been portrayed with bleak and frightening reality. The youthful gang in *A Clockwork Orange* acts brutally, without reason, without justice and without provocation, and only for the ecstasy of violence. The hero in *Straw Dogs* is a non-aggressive mathematician who has left the violence of America for the peace and tranquillity of the English countryside. His withdrawal from aggression is dramatically contrasted at the end of the movie with the excitement he finds in killing. Peckinpaw has shown that even in the gentlest of men there are passions of hostility.

Of course, many of us become ill at the sight of violence. Yet I believe that this is a learned attitude, and that man has a natural aggressive drive that needs expression, an expression that may be accompanied by ecstasy. This aggressive drive can be directed in socially acceptable and creative ways, and so be diffused before it erupts into violence.

Jerry, who had always been fearful of violence, walked through a busy downtown street one day. The bustling crowd pushed and shoved; some people seemed to go out of their way to bump him. Suddenly Jerry shoved back, and, when he did, he felt the surge of adrenalin through his body. He felt his aggression turned on and experienced the ecstasy of his hostility. This was a new and therapeutic experience for him; he experienced the pleasure of anger rather than the fear of violence.

Anger power

In the 'Here and Now' behavioural laboratory of group psychotherapy I observe people from moment to moment as they express their defiance. I often see the smile of pleasure on their faces, the sparkling of their eyes and the alerting of the muscles of their bodies. I hear the excitement in their voices as they become aware of the aliveness of their total selves. The ecstasy appears to be twofold, coming not only from the expression of anger but also from the release from the excruciating pain of anxiety and depression.

When you turn anger inwards you usually become apathetic and fatigued, and require a tremendous effort for any activity. When you turn anger outwards you become energized, with an intense flow of 'anger power' that can be used for active living and creative pursuits.

There is a real pleasure in expressing and dealing with your hostility, a definite sense of excitement, aliveness and ecstasy (almost better than the feelings from sex) in sensing your anger. I cannot give you any logical data to substantiate this. I can only ask you to test it out for yourself. I am amazed to see how many emotionally dead people become alive as they begin to ventilate their feelings of defiance and resentment. When you use your anger to solve conflicts and problems of life, your self-esteem goes up as well, and there is an accompanying feeling of well-being and enhanced personal identity. If, in handling your anger openly and directly, you do not feel pleasure, there may be several reasons. Possibly you have withdrawn or sulked to avoid some of your anger. Perhaps you have become violent, instead of verbally venting your defiance. (If you use your tongue, the chances are that you will not strike.) If we recognize the ecstasy of hostility, and the pleasure of aggression and assertive defiance, we may use it constructively to avoid the explosion of our anger into rage attacks, uncontrolled violence and destruction. We may also avoid the implosion – the turning in of anger upon ourselves that produces a range of mental illnesses, from depression to psychosomatic disorders.

Anger can be funny
Humour is an alive, healthy way of expressing your anger in a socially acceptable form. Hostile humour in my own family centres around my wife's cooking. For years I have been ribbing her about it, until our friends believe we eat only TV dinners. Some of this teasing has rubbed off on our children. One day a neighbour complained to one of my sons that our dog was eating her garbage and making a mess. He responded, 'I know. Our

dog eats your garbage because he won't eat ours. He doesn't like my mother's cooking.' Another time my wife made a gourmet meal that flopped. My daughter left the dinner table and returned a few minutes later with a neighbour whom she had just invited for supper. These anecdotes show how we ventilate our hostility through humour, and even my wife finds them funny. Do you think she gets upset? Of course not; she gets angry and exclaims, 'I will never cook again!' To which we respond in unison, 'Promises, promises, promises.'

Kick Me humour

One popular comedian, who deals completely in insult humour, said in one of his philosophical moments that it was great that we could laugh at ourselves. I wonder. Of course, much of our humour is self-directed. We poke fun at ourselves and ask other people to laugh at our mistakes. This is the 'gallows laugh'. Used in moderation, it is harmless. But a person who uses insult humour continually against himself, and really means it, may begin to suffer. After all, the 'gallows laugh' is really a form of Kick Me and may be a sign of a more malignant self-torture game.

Hammed-up humour

Another form of humour is exaggerated role response. If you detect a hidden game during an interaction, you can respond in an exaggerated way. For example, a husband asking 'Is dinner ready?' may think he sounds Adult when the tone of his voice really implies, 'Damn you, it's about time dinner was ready!' A sharp wife can pick up this game and expose it by saying, 'Oh, Your Lordship, I *am* sorry. Have I kept you waiting? I will do my best, from now on, to have food at your side at your command.' If she exaggerates enough, and the husband has some flexibility, they can break up the game with laughter. Humour in this kind of interchange is not the avoidance of genuine feelings. Rather, it is a tool used to express emotions – particularly anger – and to relate directly to someone in a meaningful way. One psychiatrist even helps his patients to study the form of such retorts – in other words, he teaches them how to use hammed-up humour to break up games that can ruin relationships.

Angry Child humour

The angry Child can be both fun and funny. Often he is vivacious, rambunctious and spirited. Humour in which we let our angry Kid out to play is very healthy and very common. One patient said at the beginning of a session, 'I feel my shit-disturbing Kid here, and I just want to mess around. It is my funny Kid and I want to play today, but I don't just want to play alone, I want to play with somebody else.' The funny Kid, when let out to play, usually hooks the funny Kids of others, and so the party begins.

Scatalogical humour is a form of angry Child humour. Jokes about the excretory system (pissing, shitting and farting) trigger explosive laughter in many people, especially young children. This kind of humour is not in itself flagrantly hostile, and it can be an indirect release of angry and aggressive feelings.

NIGYSOB *humour*

Now I've Got You, You Son of a Bitch, when played deliberately and in jest, can be a lot of fun. In this game close friends can openly criticize each other's weaknesses through laughter. Often after a squash game, my partners and I will indulge in this form of sarcasm. I might say to one of them, 'You can't run worth a damn.' And he might respond, 'Look who's talking! We used to call you the silver fox of the court, and now we just call you Fat Jack.'

A smile or laugh may be:
    an inappropriate response to unpleasantness;
    la belle indifference to a communication;
    a sign of pleasure when your needs are stroked;
    a symbol of enjoyment of your hostility;
    an indication that you are experiencing pleasure vicariously
      through the anger of others;
    the expression of the shit-disturbing, charming, wheeling-
      dealing, mischievous, angry, funny Child;

the 'Now I've got you' of the Parent ego state putting down the Child of the other fellow.

But, best of all, the smile can be the 'aha' – the pleasure of self-awareness and the excitement of personality growth.

Through anger to love: a paradox

A woman in psychotherapy began to ventilate her anger towards her husband as she placed him in the 'empty chair'. Suddenly she stopped, smiled and said, 'Hey, I wish he were here. I feel like going to bed with him, right now.'

On another occasion I was engaged in an open verbal fight with a patient in a group session. While we were shouting vigorously and expressing our irritation with each other, the patient suddenly smiled and said, 'You know, I really like you.'

It is a paradox: expressing your angry feelings frequently leads to the experiencing of the opposite feelings of warmth and love. Many couples end up making love after a vigorous fight, provided they have completed their transactions of hostility. Staying with their feelings of anger helps to liberate their emotions and to open up the spontaneous, loving Child ego state, whereas the suppression of hostility often cuts off the whole area

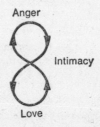

Paradox of hostility

of emotions. Showing your hostility actually allows the expression of closeness, affection, intimacy and human loving. Avoiding your anger usually results in withdrawal from friends and loss of friendship.

Silent withdrawal in marriage

Many marriages break up as a result of the partners' silent withdrawal from each other. Quiet and peaceful, this method is none the less the worst form of attempted resolution of a marriage conflict, for it eventually drains the marriage of any feeling. The husband and wife do not realize that by 'going to' each other, even with their anger, they may open up other ego states and thereby see whether affection and love still exist in the marriage. When they retreat from a fight, they lose the opportunity to work out the problem between them and they bury any remaining love.

Paper tiger

Many people are afraid to try out new behaviour patterns. They fear the consequences so much that they view any change as highly dangerous. The tragic irony is that the imagined risk usually turns out to be a paper tiger. One woman who channelled her aggressive feelings through the curse of perfectionism also had bouts of anxiety and depression. She developed intellectual awareness of her rage, but would not use it. In particular, she would not deal with her anger in her marriage relationship with a domineering and critical husband, because she feared that if she expressed her hostility he would leave her. Certainly, this was a risk. But perhaps after thirty years of marriage he would enjoy her expression of aggression and would tolerate it much better than he could tolerate her recurrent depressions and emotional incapacities.

The most common paper tiger is the fear of change itself. Old patterns of behaviour, while maladaptive and painful, are familiar and habitual. Any change holds the risk of the unknown, and tends to arouse anxiety. New tensions must be endured in the process of change and growth. If anxiety is accepted as normal, it may become the pleasurable excitement of change.

6 The conclusion

20 Growing with anger

Getting better

As you near the end of this book, what are you feeling? What are you thinking? Unfortunately you cannot answer me, so I can only guess. If you feel that 'getting better' is easy, I want to correct your impression. If you feel that all you have to do to get well is to scream, swear a bit or punch a cushion, then possibly I have misled you. However, if you feel that you can change your behaviour, that you can use your hostility to improve your communications and grow, that the techniques – although they may not be easy to employ – are quite simple to grasp, and that you can thereby alleviate your depression and improve your communication, then you have understood my message.

If I have implied that my kind of psychotherapy is the only approach to the treatment of depression, I want to clarify this. We in psychiatry are fortunate that most approaches in therapy today are very effective. Our talking treatments are generally effective, regardless of the theoretical way in which we look at depression. However, I am convinced that the new Here and Now approaches shorten the duration of illness. I think that depressions are multi-causal and have many precipitating factors, some of them chemical and others psychological. Because of this, they can be treated in different ways. Drugs, with or without psychotherapy, may be effective. The anti-depressants are effective by themselves and can help about two-thirds of all cases of depression. Electroshock is still one of the most effective treatments, but is used less today than it used to be because drugs and psychotherapy have been found to work well and are much more convenient. If you suffer from depression and none of these treatments seems to help you, remember that the depressive bouts are self-limiting. They disappear in time, although there is a tendency for them to recur.

Perhaps I have given you the impression that you can expect instantaneous breakthroughs and dramatic resolutions in the treatment of your problems. Occasionally this happens, but more often it is like finding out that you have been on the wrong road. Sometimes treatment helps you get back on the path of normal development, and even though the ride is bumpy you can proceed on your own to some satisfactory destination – 'get on with living'.

The process of change takes time, but, again, I feel that it can be faster than it used to be. It involves turmoil, pain and periods of emotional explosion. It involves meeting crises in new ways. Becoming 'normal' does not mean becoming free of pain or distress. It means learning to face crises differently, to change your relationships with people close to you, and, most important, to tolerate anxiety.

The process of change is frightening; but the greatest fear is of change itself. Our old neurotic patterns of living, while painful, are familiar. New behaviour is unknown, threatening and risky. New strains must be handled, endured and coped with in the process of growth. The paper tiger here is our fear of emotional collapse. We feel that we are too weak and vulnerable to change. Yet, regardless of our emotional disability, we are capable of tolerating the process of change and eventually reaping its rewards.

I would like to describe what 'getting better' and changing meant to one single man in his late twenties. He had been seriously ill from early adolescence with paranoid schizophrenia. For several years, he had been living a borderline existence. He felt emotionally dead and was often depressed and periodically suicidal. He maintained a very unsatisfactory job as a clerk in a government office, with a minimum of responsibility. He was bored with his work, but handled his resentment mostly by quiet withdrawal and evasion. He spent much of his time sitting in the bathroom, reading the newspaper.

When he began to undergo a period of change, he described it as a double-edged sword. He said it was like a feeling of emptiness and fragmentation. Since he really did not know who he was, it was like a period of transition; no one was to blame for his illness, and he alone had to assume responsibility for himself. He was afraid to change.

His anxiety at this time was unusually high, yet he was aware of a sense of excitement and aliveness, and he showed it in his voice. He said there was a new feeling of adventure in life, with the possibility of surprises, and a sense of independence and belief in himself that he had never had before. He found that he was able to communicate with others with greater closeness and intimacy. He was more impressed with his own ability and less concerned with what other people thought of him. He had a desire to be aggressive and assertive and to rebel, and felt that direct confrontation could be more effective than the evasive ways he had used before. He could express his feelings, instead of being restricted to intellectualizing and rationalizing.

His job became so unbearable that he left it. This created a serious problem, because he was not trained for any vocation and it was bound to be hard for him to get a new job in which he could take an interest and find some personal meaning. He might now at least be able to take some vocational training and learn a trade, but what career could he start at this point in his life? Although, job-wise, he was in a crisis, he was not quite as upset about this as he might have expected.

This period of change is one of the most tense areas of risk-taking. It is usually flooded with deep feelings of anxiety and fear of change. It is a time when the person needs help from those close to him. And, if he happens to be in therapy, he will need much support from his psychiatrist.

A young woman who was in the process of change was at an impasse. She had achieved almost total self-awareness and was able to feel her helpless, alone Child, but then she entered a period of intensive self-criticism. This feeling turned into aggressiveness and anger as her depression disappeared. The impasse she now faced centred around the question, 'Do I have the right to exist and be me?' Her fear of existing as 'me' involved the risk of being rejected. Until now she had denied herself and tried to live up to the expectations of others, but the price was recurrent depressions. Now she felt heightened anxiety as she approached diverse situations and encounters with her new script of 'I am I'.

Getting better means meeting new crises, in which there is a danger of some regression but also an opportunity for growth and pleasure. Tomorrow you may meet an old situation in which your hostility will again flare up and you will find yourself in the old reaction pattern, with either anxiety or depression – or with symptoms other than you had when you started. But remember that, besides your awareness and your experience in the realm of hostility, you also have a habit of dealing with your anger in a specific way – a pattern going back many years. The chances are that when you face another conflict the old patterns will return. If you have grown, you may find that you have some control over your behaviour. You may be able to stop the old patterns from continuing. You may be able to shorten the duration of the unpleasant symptoms. You may be able to institute new feelings and new behaviour more quickly than before. This is the 'cure': having greater freedom of choice and of response to your environment, being able to alter behaviour patterns and grow into your full potential. The more successfully you face each confrontation, the more courage you will have in facing the next step in your development.

A woman had been seriously ill for about fifteen years. She had severe obsessions and phobias, such as hand-washing compulsions. After any contact with dirt, real or imagined, she had to scrub her hands. While she recognized that her hand-washing was excessive, she was overcome by intense anxiety if she stopped it. Periods of severe depression followed. Over a period of years she tried psychotherapy and drugs; she was hospitalized several times and had repeated series of electroshock treatments, but all of the symptoms returned quite quickly. Eventually, when all else failed, she had a pre-frontal lobotomy, in which the nerve tracks in the front of the brain were cut. Despite this neuro-surgery, the same symptoms returned, and she again required hospitalization.

I met her during her last hospital bout and found her a very difficult subject for psychotherapy. She had a rigid, compulsive personality pattern, her memory was impaired, and her ability to think abstractly was poor. Yet, through simple psychotherapy, she began to learn to express her hostility. Today, five years after leaving the hospital, she has learned the lesson well. Of course, she has had recurrent symptoms, but they subside quite quickly. She requires tranlquilizers and anti-depressants, but, generally, she is living a productive and almost symptom-free life.

Recently, in therapy, she told me a simple story that probably was not very significant to anyone except her. It symbolized many years of suffering. A devout Roman Catholic, she had been visited a few days before by another woman from her church, who severely criticized her for not sending her son to a particular church function. My patient 'told the woman off' and enjoyed every moment of it. She said that she could not have done this fifteen years ago, and through all of the therapy in the past no one had ever taught her to be angry. What a terrible illness she had suffered before she learned this simple lesson of showing her hostility: When? Now. Where? Here.

Free to grow again

In writing this book on hostility, I started by introducing the subject and myself. Then I described the faces of anger, the encounters with hostility in a general way as revealed in day-to-day living. Next I showed how the outward signs of depression, anxiety and perfectionism are often masks to hide the anger that exists, avoided or undetected, within the individual. After that, I explored with you the Me Too, the stroke-demanding, dependent part of the Child ego state that I have found to lie at the root of many people's hostile feelings. Finally, in this last section, I have sought to show how these ideas can best be applied, here and now. Throughout the book I have drawn upon experiences in my psychiatric practice to illustrate or underline certain points.

We have seen that anger turned inwards leads to feelings of inferiority, to depression, anxiety and brooding, to the carrying around of resentments, to incomplete encounters and to poor social relations. Anger directed outwards, on the other hand, leads to assertiveness, increased self-worth, and improved personal and social relationships. In this way your anger can be dissipated and the encounters in your life completed. Not only does the constructive handling of your hostility help to solve emotional problems in the present; it can be an on-going process of growth in the future.

In the mental health field today, we are talking differently than we did in the past when we were preoccupied with 'getting over' illness and removing neurosis. We are now talking about growing into your full personality potential. Many of us live within a very narrow scope of personality. (It has been estimated that most people utilize only five to fifteen per cent of their personality potential.) Frequently, when we meet problems, we contrive to remain comfortable by avoiding and cutting off part of our personality, such as the scared Kid.

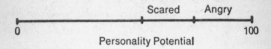

We may avoid feeling anxious by doing this, but we also lose that part of our personality. We may not feel hurt, but we are in fact limiting the breadth and scope of our personalities and of our relationships with others, as well as our total potential for living. By recognizing and reowning hidden and rejected parts of yourself – especially your angry self – you open up previously untapped areas of your personality. I myself found that, by accepting the 'bastard' in myself (even while I was writing this book), I began to get in touch with a sense of sarcastic humour that I had hidden for many years.

Full growth of the personality potential involves the sensing, the liberation and the use of all of the roles of the Parent, Adult and Child ego states. The word 'role' is not used here in a phony or dramatic sense, and means an actual part of the real self. For example, the Child ego state has various roles that are interdependent. Getting in touch with one part frequently frees others. It is my opinion that the dependent Me Too Child is the core of the Child ego state. The anger that results from the frustration of our basic needs is a universal reaction that can be used in a rewarding way, even adaptively, to resolve hostile-dependent conflicts. Opening up the dependent and angry ego parts releases other roles which can then contribute to personality growth. The healthy, autonomous individual exhibits flexibility, a rhythm of change, a freedom of flow through all the

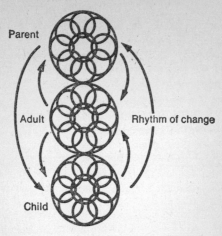

Parent

Adult

Rhythm of change

Child

The total self — multiple roles in each ego state

roles of his ego states, in response to the changing problems and crises of daily living.

As I have shown throughout this book, an awareness of your anger on the level of feeling, the acceptance of your resentments by your conscience, and the expression of your hostility by your Adult ego state in the here and now can dissolve conflicts, open communications, relieve neuroses, and clear the way for growth towards your full personality potential. The creative, spontaneous, alive and intuitive aspects of your personality can emerge. You can uncover your hidden resources of pleasure, sexiness, warmth and affection. You can relate to others in a genuine, trusting, intimate, loving way.

Afterword

I was not involved in Transactional Analysis (although I had read Eric Berne's books) until I attended a workshop in it led by John Cooper of Carmel, California. John's charm and warmth made Eric Berne's ideas come alive, and I was hooked. I then made a number of trips to California for training in Transactional Analysis at the Western Institute for Group and Family Therapy. There, under Bob Goulding, the director, and his wife Mary, I took an exciting professional and personal journey through Transactional Analysis and Gestalt Therapy *à la* Goulding. Many of my basic concepts are derived from Bob's ideas on Transactional Analysis, and this book has developed from these concepts and from my experience as a clinical psychiatrist.

I have learned from many sources, but primarily from workshops and from lectures by outstanding people in the profession: Alexander Lowen, Everett Shostrom, Rollo May, Harry Harlow, Albert Ellis, Jorge Rosner and Eric Berne, and through the movies of Fritz Perls. Harvey Freedman, a Gestalt therapist and one of my 'Y' colleagues, has shared his ideas, and he supported me during my pains and frustrations as an emerging Here and Now psychotherapist. Bill Halloway, a close friend, colleague and teacher, has helped clarify my thinking in Transactional Analysis. Pam Joho of General Publishing Company and Tom Fairley have been great working companions. Many friends have read my manuscript and given me their opinions, including Bill Allen, Tom Verny, Jerry Friedland, Mel Hundert, Clifford Nelson, Ruth Glicksman and Ruben Schafer. Ken McBride edited the book and Marianne Friedland gave much valuable literary and editorial assistance. My secretary, Rose Matthews, has done much more than manuscript typing by being a warm friend and an excellent colleague. My wife, Sally, and my children, Mike, Leslie, Peter and David, have always shown an excited interest in my work and have voiced their opinions, which do not always coincide with mine. I also want to thank my patients, whose responses and efforts to help themselves have, more than anything else, stimulated my professional growth and the creation of this book. Last but not least I want to stroke myself – 'Good work, Jack!'

Suggested reading

TRANSACTIONAL ANALYSIS

BERNE, Eric. *Games People Play*. Deutsch, 1966.

BERNE, Eric. *Principles of Group Treatment*. Oxford University Press, 1966.

BERNE, Eric. *Sex in Human Loving*. Deutsch, 1971; Penguin, 1973.

BERNE, Eric. *Transactional Analysis in Psychotherapy*. Evergreen Books, 1961.

BERNE, Eric. *What Do You Say after You Say Hello?* Deutsch, 1974.

HARRIS, Thomas A. *I'm OK – You're OK: A Practical Guide to Transactional Analysis*. Cape, 1973; Pan, 1973.

JAMES, Muriel, and JONGEWARD, Dorothy. *Born to Win*. Addison-Wesley Publishing Co, 1971.

SCHIFT, Jacqui Lee. *All My Children*. New York: M. Evans & Co Inc, 1970.

STEINER, Claude. *Games Alcoholics Play: The Analysis of Life Scripts*. New York: Grove Press Inc, 1971.

GESTALT THERAPY

FAGAN, Joen, and SHEPHERD, Irma Lee, eds. *Gestalt Therapy Now*. Penguin, 1972.

PERLS, Frederick S. *Gestalt Therapy Verbatim*. Bantam Books, 1972.

PERLS, Frederick S. *In and Out of the Garbage Pail*. Bantam Books, 1973.

MISCELLANEOUS

RADO, Sandor, *Psychoanalysis of Behaviour*. Vol 1. New York: Grune and Stratton, 1956.

REICH, Charles A. *The Greening of America*. Allen Lane, 1971; Penguin, 1972.

SPITZ, René A. 'Anaclitic Depression'. *Psychoanalytic Study of the Child*. 2:313-42, 1946.

Index

Peter Blythe
Stress – The Modern Sickness 60p

Why is stress an ever-increasing problem? How does the mind convert stress into physical illness? When can stress lead to a broken marriage? Is being over-weight a stress symptom?

These and many other vital questions are discussed by Peter Blythe, a practising psychotherapist and consultant hypnotist, who examines every aspect of normal living and shows where the build-up of anxiety-stress-tension plays a determining part in a variety of illnesses.

Dr Joan Gomez
How Not to Die Young 70p

Are you living dangerously?

With the aid of two hundred and forty practical, multi-choice questions, Dr Gomez indicates the many different actions and dangerous habits which could do your health irrevocable harm, and shows how unnecessary deaths can be avoided.

Mildred Nemman and Bernard Berkowitz
How to be Your Own Best Friend 35p

This remarkable book, written with warmth, understanding and wisdom, provides simple guidelines to help you become the person it is in you to be.

'There is no pill made that is as simple, effective and fast-working . . . positively inspirational' NEIL SIMON

William Sargant
The Mind Possessed 75p

A riveting investigation into possession – by demons, gods, drugs, sex or religion – which gives an enthralling insight into the human mind. Dr William Sargant, famous author of *Battle for the Mind*, here relates his fascinating experiences as he studied the phenomenon of possession all over the world – casting out devils in Ethiopia . . . voodooism in Haiti . . . smoke-induced possession in Zambia . . . religious revival meetings in America . . . From these studies – many of them experienced at first hand – Dr Sargant raises crucial questions about us and our minds . . .

Michael Allaby with Marika Hanbury-Tenison,
John Seymour & Hugh Sharman
**The Survival Handbook – Self-Sufficiency
for Everyone** £1.25

Founded on the authors' long experience, this invaluable handbook
gives sensible and detailed information – illustrated with many drawings
– on how to be self-sufficient; and how individuals, families and larger
communities can create a richer life.

Subjects covered include: building a house, from foundations to roof;
making one's own furniture, pottery, soap and candles; spinning, dyeing
and weaving; farming and gardening – and food for free.

Sheila Moore
Working For Free 75p

In this sensible, practical and comprehensive guide Sheila Moore details
a multitude of opportunities for voluntary work. These include *Social
Work* in hospitals, prisons, with the elderly and the handicapped;
Political Activity in national and local government; *Fund Raising* and how
to do this successfully. The author also advises on how to choose one's
voluntary work; whom to contact; what to expect – and what *not* to
expect.